D1667379

SELF~HELP PROMOTION

a challenge to the NGO community

Koenraad Verhagen

CEBEMO / Royal Tropical Institute
The Netherlands

This publication is an integrated report of a study conducted by three non-governmental organizations in Brazil, Indonesia and Thailand, coordinated by CEBEMO, on the promotion of economic activities in rural areas. The responsibility for the opinions expressed rests solely with the author, and their publication does not constitute an endorsement thereof by the joint publishers, Cebemo and the Royal Tropical Institute, nor by any of the Cebemo counterpart organizations which have participated in the study.

Cebemo is a Dutch organization for development co-operation, which, on behalf of the Dutch Catholic Community, acts as a channel of the joint financing programme of the Dutch Government. Cebemo finances initiatives of a developmental nature at grassroot level.
The basis of the activities of the *Royal Tropical Institute* is the collection and dissemination of knowledge in tropical countries, concentrated in three main programmes: rural development, tropical hygiene and transfer of knowledge. The relevant development projects in these fields are carried out preferably in combination with scientific research, education and training.

Self-help promotion, a challenge to the NGO community is the first publication in the new series of the Royal Tropical Institute *STUDIES IN RURAL DEVELOPMENT*.

Cebemo
Rhijngeesterstraatweg 40
2341 BV OEGSTGEEST
The Netherlands

Koninklijk Instituut voor de Tropen (KIT)
Royal Tropical Institute
Mauritskade 63
1092 AD AMSTERDAM
The Netherlands

CIP-GEGEVENS KONINKLIJKE BIBLIOTHEEK, DEN HAAG

Verhagen, Koenraad

Self-help promotion: a challenge to the NGO Community: integrated report of a study conducted by three non-governmental organizations in Brazil, Indonesia and Thailand, coordinated by CEBEMO, on the promotion of economic activities in rural areas / Koenraad Verhagen. – Amsterdam: Koninklijk Instituut voor de Tropen; Oegstgeest: Cebemo. – Ill., fig., tab. – (Studies in rural development)
Met bibliogr., index, reg.
ISBN 90 6832 019 X
SISO 354.7 UDC [339.96:631/632](81+594+593)
Trefw.: landbouw; ontwikkelingssamenwerking; Brazilië/landbouw; ontwikkelingssamenwerking; Indonesië/landbouw; ontwikkelingssamenwerking; Thailand.

© 1987 – Royal Tropical Institute, Amsterdam/Cebemo, Oegstgeest
Cover design – Freek Thielsch, Amsterdam
ISBN 90 6832 019 X
NUGI 659
Distributed outside the Netherlands by
Foris Publications, P.O. Box 509
3000 AM Dordrecht – the Netherlands

Printed in the Netherlands by ICG Printing, Dordrecht

Table of contents

Foreword

Before you is a book, which is the result of a lot of research, reflection and discussion. It may therefore seem to be a final report, but that is not exactly the case. Of course this report is now finalized, but the process of action and reflection on how to encourage economic activities in rural areas will continue both within Cebemo and the intermediary organizations with whom Cebemo cooperates, i.e. Cebemo's partner organizations in the developing countries. Fortunately, Cebemo was not the only one to be working along these lines throughout the whole exercise, for a similar research had been started earlier in West Germany (BMZ, S24/ES 31). This facilitated the starting up in Cebemo, whilst the Germans were able to profit from the contribution and geographical spread of the Dutch research. This resulted in a fruitful and exemplary cooperation, also at the personal level, between the various researchers and their supervisory teams. There were certain differences however. Whereas the research initiated in Germany concentrated on the financial instrumentarium, the research in the Netherlands devoted more attention to the relation between the intermediary structure and the target groups.

Right from the start, it was clear that for the type of study to be undertaken most of the research work would have to be done in the field. It was also clear that, for such research to be fruitful, it could only be carried out by Cebemo's partners in the Third World, while Cebemo provided coordination and methodological guidance in order to guarantee that the various results would be comparable. For this latter aspect, expertise was found in the Netherlands. Cebemo feels fortunate to have been assisted by an outstanding resource person with great research experience in the Third World, especially concerning cooperatives and other similar types of organizations. The Royal Tropical Institute was willing to put this person at Cebemo's disposal for the lengthy period necessary to the research. Once the terms of reference for the research were formulated, an agreement was soon reached with the partners on the set-up and methodology of the work to be done. The thorough way in which this was subsequently carried out has been very striking, especially as this work came as an addition to their many other daily tasks.

The rounding off of the first part of the process took place at the workshop held in Oegstgeest followed by the approval by the researchers of the final report. Cebemo is very pleased with the findings and will have to see how the results can influence our work here. As for the partner organizations in Brazil, Indonesia and Thailand, the research has also led to adjustments both regarding policies and methods used.

The report furnishes some useful entry points for further follow-up but does not (and cannot) have the pretention to provide a solution for all concrete cases. Cebemo will now enter a second phase, together with sister organizations in the Netherlands, together also with other similar organizations in the developed countries, but especially and mainly with her partners in the Third World.

I wish to end with an expression of thanks to Bina Swadaya, CCTD, CERIS, MOC and the DISACs involved in the research for all the efforts devoted to this process; and also a word of thanks to the Task Force – and Pieter Damen in particular – in which many people from different disciplines and backgrounds participated and often made useful contributions. Of course the external financing from the RABO and the Ministry of Development Cooperation in the Netherlands (DPO) was also most welcome, for without this the research would have exceeded Cebemo's financial means.
Finally I would like to thank the author for his creativity, perseverance and dedication.
We hope this report may therefore contribute in many places to obtaining more insight in the issues of development in rural areas in the Third World and in the role which the intermediary and financing organizations may play.

Hans Kruijssen,
Cebemo General Director

Acknowledgements

A study of this type cannot be conducted without the efforts of many people. There is not room to mention everyone but we would particularly like to thank the authors and coordinators of the three studies in Brazil, Indonesia and Thailand which have formed the basis for this book, and also those who participated in the follow-up Consultation which took place in September 1986 in Oegstgeest: Ildes de Oliveira, João Cicero de Souza Aloes, José Carlos de Santana Souza from Brazil; Bambang Ismawan, Methodius Kusumahadi, Panut Wiyarto, and Heinz Bongartz from Indonesia; Dr. Kanjana Kaewthep, Dr. Kanoksak Kaewthep, Fr. Vacharin Samanchit, Fr. Nipot Thienviharn and Tu Sornchai from Thailand. Thanks are also due to my Cebemo colleagues who have actively contributed to the study's progress in various capacities: first the members of the Cebemo Task Force, especially Vincent Brenninkmeijer, its secretary, for his unfailing practical and moral back-up, as well as the other Cebemo members, Tony Fernandes, our skilful 'moderator' during the Consultation Meeting, and also Joris Biemans, Nico van Niekerk, Wim Peeters and Jaap van Soest for their incisive and helpful comments. Ben Krommendijk, Guido Hilhorst and Theo Janssen as country experts provided invaluable advice at different stages of the study. Our gratitude also goes to Carla Houben for reporting the Consultation's proceedings, to Lia v.d. Craats for skilful typing and checking of an impressive number of Working Documents and interim papers, and Javier Ferreira Ramos for his effective assistance during the report's last stage of production. Meine Pieter van Dijk of the Royal Tropical Institute, Doede Wind of the Rabobank and Theo Kolstee of the Netherlands' Ministry of Foreign Affairs have all very constructively participated in the Task Force proceedings. Substantial financial assistance was received from the Ministry of Foreign Affairs for conducting the study and the Rabobank has generously contributed to the holding of the Consultation Meeting with our overseas counterparts.
While the successful completion of the study was unthinkable without the contributions of the above mentioned individuals and organizations, we would like to record here our special thanks to the study's skilful coordinator and author of the book, Koenraad Verhagen, for his never failing enthusiasm and dedication to work.

Pieter Damen,
Chairman of the Task Force

7

Author's preface

Since the existence of mankind, self-help has been practised in innumerable ways. Even today, it is the main characteristic of the productive behaviour of the rural poor. Past developmental approaches of techno-scientific inspiration have largely ignored this potential. They have facilitated the introduction of new systems of organization and production which tend to undercut rather than stimulate the capacity of the rural poor to help themselves.

While modern times have provided greater opportunities for the few, they have narrowed the economic base of the 'poor majority' living in the rural areas of Brazil, Thailand and Indonesia where the present study was undertaken. Similar observations can be made in relation to the position of the rural poor in other developing countries where over the past decades their status has been reduced to that of 'beneficiaries' of development projects, 'adopters' of new technologies, consumers of ill-coordinated public welfare services, day labourers, plantation or factory workers, etc., situations which all imply a high degree of dependence on the benevolence, entrepreneurial capacities and economic means of others than themselves.

It has now become commonplace to say that national economic growth alone cannot prevent the growth of mass poverty. In fact, the one-sided emphasis on economic achievement by national policy-makers has set in motion a process of alarming socio-economic polarization and the deepening of social cleavages in both urban and rural areas (see El Ghonemy, 1985; and Rahman Kahn and Lee, 1984, for factual information and analysis). Since the rural poor have become too numerous to be helped from outside, 'self-help' has emerged as a new paradigm for combating rural poverty, and 'self-help promotion' as the main orientation for local NGOs in developing countries. The promising experiences of some of them have prompted German development agencies to take up the self-help concept as a major issue for documentation and discussion (Osner et al., 1984; DSE, 1985). From a political perspective, the NGOs' involvement in the promotion of self-help and economic activities is a sensitive issue and their relationship to government initiatives has become an important subject of national and international debate (OECD, 1986; van Dijk, 1986; Tongsawate and Tips, 1985; Hendrata Lukas, 1983). The complexity of the subject is further illustrated by the cases discussed in this report.

8

Given the negative socio-economic effects of ongoing macro-processes, the basic question is whether these can be counteracted effectively by micro-initiatives undertaken with NGO support. This study cannot give a definite answer to that question. It can only offer a perspective of hope, just as the economic activities themselves do to an increasing number of rural poor.

This study will review an approach in NGO development work which endeavours to

widen the scope of autonomous action for the rural poor, and enables them to acquire more latitude in steering socio-economic change in a direction consistent with their own priorities and long-term interests. Two key elements in this approach are:
– building upon what the rural poor have, rather than what they lack;
– facilitating and promoting their organization.

The study was initiated by Cebemo. The local NGOs in the three countries which decided to participate in the study venture, did so while acknowledging the fact that they have a lot of experience in self-help promotion, but that the circumstances under which they work leave them little opportunity to reflect in a systematic way on their experiences. Their participation in the study offered a welcome opportunity to dig deeper into the analysis of certain questions which they consider vital for the achievement of their objectives. The participant NGOs were based in three different countries: Brazil, Indonesia and Thailand. In Brazil, the study was undertaken by MOC (Movimento de Organizaçao Comunitaria, Feira de Santana) with the backing-up of CERIS, Rio de Janeiro; in Indonesia, by Bina Swadaya (Jakarta); and in Thailand, by two DISACs (Diocesan Social Action Centres) with support from their apex organization, the CCTD, Bangkok.

The present report is divided into two parts. The first part, comprising Chapters 1 to 4, is concerned with the premises, concepts and methodology of the study. Conceived in broad terms at the beginning of the study, these have been further refined, developed and adjusted in the course of the study as a result of the ongoing dialogue with the participant organizations in the three countries and contributions from members of the Cebemo Task Force.

The first part of the book has deliberately been written in such a way that it can be used in its own right as a discussion and working document for any organization considering the possibility of undertaking a study of comparable nature and focus. It therefore ends with a discussion of 'problems encountered' by the participant NGOs while conducting the study from which important lessons can be drawn (Chapter 4). The second part of the book, Chapters 5 to 10, reports the 'study findings and conclusions'. It is a synthesis and re-interpretation of the studies carried out in the three countries. The operations of local NGOs, termed Self-help Promotion Institutions (SHPIs), are reviewed, together with their interaction with Self-Help Organizations (SHOs) and the performance of the latter, as part of an overall system of self-help promotion. In this process an important conditioning factor is the role played by foreign funding agencies. Therefore the second part of Chapter 9, will consider the implications of the study for the modus operandi of such agencies. The greater number of pages devoted to analysis of the Brazilian SHOs can be explained by the greater variety and complexity of their operations, while the treatment of the Thai case has been augmented by a special section on the 'holistic' approach because of its originality (Chapter 9 – first part).

The field studies were conducted during the second half of 1985 and early 1986 over a five to six months' period in each country. Subsequent to the production of the three country reports and a preliminary version of the present integrated report, a 'Consultation' was held during the first two weeks of September 1986 in The Netherlands. The Consultation provided an opportunity for researchers and representatives of the participating local NGOs to review and compare their respective study findings and follow-up programmes, and to discuss their development strategies and perspectives intensively with Cebemo staff. The proceedings of the Consultation and the follow-up programmes presented by the participating NGOs are the subject of separate documents. (Cebemo 1986a and 1986b).

Maps showing the research areas

Location of research area, Gunung Kidul District, in the Special Territory (Province) of Yogyakarta, Java.

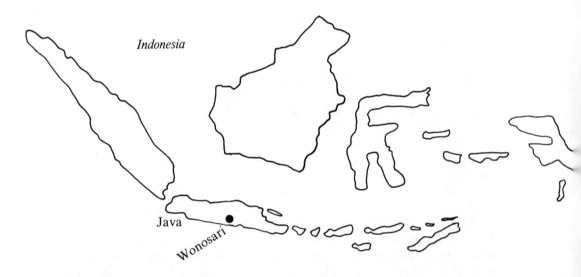

Part I

Premises, objectives, conceptual framework

Location of research areas, Sisaket Province in the northeast and Chomthong District near the city of Chiengmai in north Thailand.

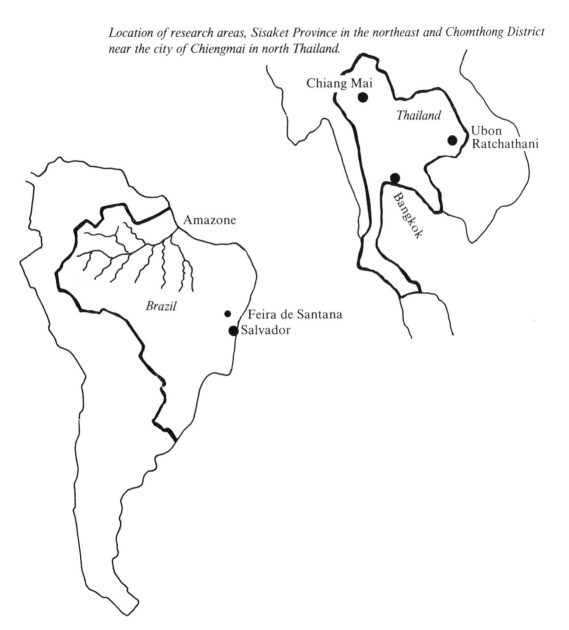

Location of research area, Serrinha 'Municipio' (District) in the State of Bahia, northeast Brazil.

1 Theoretical basis for self-help promotion

Misguided concepts in development practice

If we want to make our assistance more effective in strengthening the economy of the poor, we should start where some of the roots of the problem lie: that is within our own organizations and within our own minds where we tend to cherish ideas and assumptions which may provide legitimacy to our work, help secure the survival of our own organizations, but prohibit a consistent approach to self-help promotion among the rural poor. Self-help promotion has to start with a critical examination of the assumptions upon which earlier development efforts were based, and most of the ongoing efforts still are. General notions such as: development agencies have fulfilled their tasks when they have 'reached the poor'; creating new employment is good in itself; because the poor are unemployed, they are also underoccupied; the poor cannot save; we need more money for more projects, are mainly of technocratic inspiration. They are the products of a system of thought and reasoning, characteristic of the outsider's vision of change and attitude towards development issues. In an insidious way, they tend to steer our thinking in the direction of top-down interventions and disregard of the people's own ambitions and potential for self-help.

It is true that there is no such thing as a single system of thought and reasoning attached to development organizations which is commonly adhered to by all the people concerned. Yet there is a form of conventional wisdom which upon closer analysis may prove to be more conventional than wise, and which does not favour, and may even obstruct, the promotion of self-help among the rural poor. The five short statements and comments below challenge such wisdom and provided the rationale for the undertaking of a study on self-help.

–The issue is not how we can 'reach the poor'
By 'being reached' the position of the poor may be weakened, not strengthened. By merely 'being reached' the poor tend to become dependent on the feeding bottles of development agencies, and encapsulated in a development process not of their own making. There are great risks that the poor in their role of 'beneficiaries' may become overly dependent on their benefactors for delivery of inputs, access to credit, sale of produce, or other facilities, and may finally be left in a very vulnerable position. This is not to say that the established development agencies with distributory functions have no role to play. They have, but in a supportive and not in a directive function. Self-help organization is a means of raising the claim-making capacity of the rural poor for reaching out to such agencies as they are willing to work with, and which can provide them with additional production resources. It also implies the development of their bargaining power to an extent that such agencies cannot unilaterally impose their conditions and regulations upon the rural poor as passive recipients, but that the

13

terms and conditions of collaboration are the outcome of a process of negotiation in which both parties are respectful of each other's priorities and specific interests. The Thai study is particularly illustrative of the capacity of self-help groups to rise to a level where they can accept government assistance without having to submit themselves to conditions which do not fit their situation. At the same time, we should be mindful of the fact that to feed that process, the poor may need the assistance of outsiders, persons who, in that process, perform catalytic and promotional functions until such time as the poor are sufficiently organized to claim their own economic, social and political rights. These are the temporary functions to be performed by the type of organizations central to this study: Self-Help Promotion Institutions (SHPIs).

– Creating 'new employment opportunities' has no value in itself
More employment opportunities in general should be welcomed. But this offers no key to the problem of rural poverty if it leaves the employee no other choice than to accept a minimal return for his work, just enough to survive, but too much to die. In most developing countries we find a situation of abundant supply of cheap labour, while economic growth is stagnant and insufficiently labour-intensive to absorb an ever-growing rural labour force. Under such conditions employment creation does not do much to raise standards of living as long as the poor cannot exercise any control over conditions of work and distribution of benefits. There is something extraordinarily comtemptuous and humiliating in the argument that the best way to help the poor is to increase the production opportunities of the more powerful national and local entrepreneurs in the hope that bigger and better crumbs will fall from the rich men's tables. Self-help promotion does not accept such a cynical premise and attempts to raise the level of voice of the poor majority in the economic system by the build-up of an institutional framework that is tuned to their capacities of self-administration and better geared towards serving their needs.

– Many rural poor are 'unemployed' – yet they are over-occupied
Budget studies of poor households, including those undertaken under the present study, show that household members contribute to the household income, in cash or in kind, from the proceeds of a great variety of occupations, some of them on the brink of legality. These may include farming, fishing, small trade, wage labour, handicrafts, small-scale processing, collecting firewood, carrying water, etc. Employed or self-employed, the poor endure very long working days and must use all their energy, ingenuity and entrepreneurial skill to reach a level of material welfare which permits survival. 'Unemployed' or 'underemployed' is a somewhat strange label for people who feel they are over-burdened and over-occupied.* However, what all these occupations have in common is the low level of net income, in kind or in cash, which they provide compared to the input of labour, time and energy.**

14

*As some critics of the study pointed out, over-occupation may not be present in all developing situations, and is often seasonal. It is more frequent and intense among women than among men.
**'While the return on labour in the agricultural sector is already very low, many studies prove that the return on labour in off-farming sectors is even lower' (Indonesian Study, p. 3).

Self-help promotion as a development approach tries to build upon this existing self-help potential of the rural poor and assist them as producers, and in the identification of occupations and activities which provide a higher net return on invested labour and capital. Complementary to this, as consumers, they may get better value for their money by buying from a cooperative consumer shop (Brazilian case study).

– The poor have productive resources
By conceiving poverty as a condition of 'not having', or 'not being able', we tend to forget what the poor possess and are capable of doing. By dramatizing their deprivations, we tend to forget what they have. The poor are not 'have-nots'. From a purely economic point of view, they are 'have little'. They have for example, as demonstrated by many studies, a saving potential which can be used for capital formation (ILO, 1983; Osner et al., 1984); they have detailed knowledge of their immediate environment and development constraints; they often have a piece of land; most are sufficiently able-bodied for a substantial labour input, and they have some technical and entrepreneurial skills and capacity for self-organization. Without all this, they would not be able to survive in an opportunistic capitalist environment. Moreover, the poor have their own social and cultural wealth, a point which all action-researchers involved in this study have not failed to emphasize and which often puts them at the receiving end in a learning process. What the poor lack, however, is sufficient opportunity to widen and diversify their resource-basis. Through self-help organizations, they may be able to acquire access to some complementary non-material resources (knowledge, skills) as well as some material ones (credit, raw material, land, water, etc).

– Present systems of project financing are not conducive to people's participation
Development agencies, be they 'donor' or 'recipient', both have difficulties in adopting an 'open-ended' or 'non-project approach' such as recommended by a recent CEC Evaluative Study (Crombrugge, Howes & Nieuwkerk, 1985). Having assessed the somewhat disappointing performance of 25 CEC-financed small development projects, the study team argues for much more flexible systems of financing and devolution of powers to the lower levels of development administration. Eventually, this should lead 'to an open-ended approach in which no initial limit is placed upon the range of options that might be considered' p. 45). The recommendation in itself is not new, but is important because of the significant NGO component in the projects which were analysed. It exemplifies the difficulties private organizations, too, have in concretizing a philosophy of facilitating more endogenous types of development. In principle most NGOs favour self-help and 'people's participation'; in practice they are faced with administrative and organizational constraints which inhibit the full materialization of self-help at grassroots level. One of these constraints is the project approach which in reality proves difficult to reconcile with a process of organic growth, i.e. a natural process of growth and expansion, from small to larger, which receives its inspiration and direction chiefly from the needs and aspirations of the rural poor, as and when they present themselves. The loss of flexibility which the conventional project approach entails was vividly expressed by a Brazilian action-researcher who said: 'Once you have got the money from the donor agency, you have become the prisoner of your own plan'.

The reluctance to discard the 'project approach' can be explained from different angles. First, it is against the administrative tradition which views development processes as technical processes. The underlying assumption is that if projects are well designed and implemented, they will yield predictable outputs from a given set of project inputs. Self-help organizations, however, develop their own momentum. The direction they will take cannot be predicted by outsiders. Inputs certainly should produce outputs, but not necessarily those which administrators, technicians or benefactors regard as priorities. Secondly, an agency's financial commitment to an 'open-ended' programme causes insecurity about future claims for financial and technical assistance at the donor and intermediate levels of the funding chain. It also entails uncertainty about the moneys to be spent, the timing of disbursements and repayments, and the duration of the assistance. Finally, self-help promotion among the rural poor is financially not attractive for organizations which cover their operational costs from a fixed or negotiated proportion of their project money turnover. Self-help by definition has a limited absorption capacity for outside assistance, especially in the initial stages of group formation and cooperative action. The assumption that the administrative criteria and procedures which regulate the functioning of the international aid system hamper rather than facilitate self-help promotion, was confirmed by the present study, although this was not its focus. However, the matter has also come up as a subject for further investigation and as a possible follow-up to the present study. Preliminary conclusions in this respect are presented in Chapter 9, following a more detailed analysis of the self-help promotion strategies of the participant NGOs in the earlier chapters.

The poor majority

Who are the rural poor with whom this study is concerned? Poverty is a relative concept and, by implication, highly contextual. The poor are not a homogeneous fraction of society, they can be divided into various categories according to the cause of poverty, degree, outward manifestations (such as food habits or poor housing), sex and age and other environmental characteristics. For the definition of poverty, the present study has followed the most obvious criteria as suggested by the specific setting in which the study took place and with a focus on poor households rather than individuals. In all such cases, the possession of, and access to, land carried great weight, as it lays the foundation for other inequalities and differences in opportunities.

In *Brazil*, the chief criterion used was identical to the one used by the organization for small farmers and agricultural labourers (APAEB) which was at the centre of the Brazilian study. Farmers who employ agricultural labourers on a regular basis are barred from the organization's membership. Farmers, male or female, who cannot do so because of the smaller size of their farms, and landless agricultural workers are considered as poor. The better-off among these poor possess what is known internationally as a 'family farm' (providing work for two adults and two children). The greater part of their farmland (about 10 hectares) is normally used as grazing grounds. Movement leadership also mostly originates from this section of what can be regarded as the upper rank of the rural poor. The majority of the members are far below this average and scratch their subsistence from a much smaller piece of land (on average 3 hectares), or they are landless and completely dependent upon wage labour. The poor so defined together constitute 96% of the rural households in the research area (Serrinha district).

In *Indonesia*, the SHO members living in the more affluent quarters of the first village cluster, Baleharjo, with an annual cash income per household of $2,000 to $4,000, almost entirely from non-agricultural activities (e.g. teaching, trading) were not regarded as belonging to the rural poor. Households (six to seven members) with an annual income of less than $1000 – which was the case for nearly all households living in the second village cluster Pacing – were considered as rural poor. Landlessness in that part of Java is rare, but land parcels are small to very small (under 0.5 hectare often in tenancy).

As in Brazil and Thailand, participation by the poor in SHO activities tends to diminish with the degree of poverty.

Similarly, landholdings in the *North Thailand* research area are also small (between 0.3 and 1.3 hectares), often cultivated under tenancy, and able to produce two crops per year. Landlessness however is high (in some places over 50%). The entire village population of the research location could be ranked under one of two categories, small farmer or landless, and was considered to belong to the rural poor. In the other research location in Thailand the average landholding amounts to 4.8 hectares (single crop) which is high even by Northeast standards. But because of the poor quality of the soil, few are surplus farmers. Those who are, and those who regularly employ labourers were not regarded as poor for the purposes of the study. In this the villagers' perception was followed. These people also chose to refrain from participation in SHO activities (see Chapter 7).

Though land may be an important criterion for classification, it should be realized that most of the income of the rural poor in the research locations is earned from wage labour and other off-farm occupations. (For more details on living and working conditions of the rural poor and their environment, see Part II, Chapter 5, 'Research areas and villages' and Chapter 8 'Identification of target population and self-help groups').

The associative economy in perspective

The three-sector economy

Self-help organizations (SHOs) are membership organizations since they are administered and controlled by their members, whose interests they are supposed to serve. Membership organizations are meant to counterbalance the overwhelming influence on the economy of the profit-oriented private sector and the state-controlled public sector. When functioning according to their principles, they offer the poor an opportunity for a partial re-shaping of the economic system which governs their daily lives in a direction congruent with their interests. Membership organizations together constitute the associative sector of the economy , in short the associative economy. The notion of this three-sector system can be illustrated as follows*:

* Design adjusted from the Thai report, p. 13.

Figure 1: The three-sector economic system

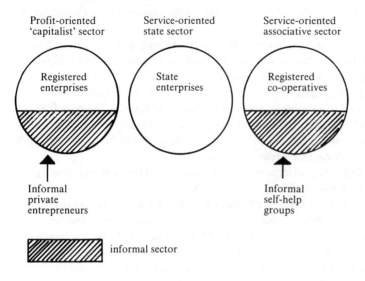

Profit-oriented 'capitalist' sector	Service-oriented state sector	Service-oriented associative sector
Registered enterprises	State enterprises	Registered co-operatives
Informal private entrepreneurs		Informal self-help groups

informal sector

For conceptual clarity it is important to distinguish the informal sector from the associative sector. Informal, unregistered forms of small-scale enterprise are found in both the profit-oriented sector and the associative sector of the economy. The self-employed street vendor or peddler or seamstress operates in the first sector, small unregistered self-help groups in the third, associative sector. The sectors are not mutually exclusive but complementary. They belong to a single unified economic system.

The associative sector and its constituent economic undertakings can be viewed as the material expression of an 'alternative economy' (MOC, Development Plan 1986). MOC in this context refers specifically to the cooperatively managed units for common storage, processing, sale of consumer goods, etc., which are owned by and directly serve the needs of the under-privileged sections of society, and to the exchange of goods and services between those units. It is an evolutionary rather than a revolutionary scenario, even if, in the long term, more drastic changes are pursued (land reform in the Brazilian case).

It should be emphasized that the development of an associative sector in itself is unable to solve problems of rural poverty or to change positively the position of low-income groups, if the structure of the organization's membership is predominantly high and middle income (Verhagen, 1984, pp. 6-8 and 117-130). In fact, cooperatives and similar types of organization may even worsen the contradictions in rural areas where they are successful in creating new opportunities for the 'haves' and simultaneously reduce the opportunities for, or neglect the interests of, the 'have-little'. Where this tends to happen we may, however, at the same time see the emergence of associative forms of organization among the rural poor whose success can be attributed to their effectiveness in counterbalancing trends of 'centralized authoritarianism and capitalist exploitation' (Cendhrra, 1982, p. 9).

There is indeed sufficient, documented, empirical evidence available now to show that the poor, under a wide variety of circumstances, are able to bring about substantial improvements in their living conditions through self-help effort. Such 'success cases' of self-help or similar forms of organization as well as general conditions of success are amply described in development literature (see for example Osner et al., 1985; Rouille d'Orfeuil, 1984; Esman and Uphoff, 1984). These studies describe and analyze cases which have been going on for many years and are different in their expression, but identical in their substance. The discussion will not be repeated here.

In self-help promotion economic growth, too, is one of the aims. But not the kind of growth which exploits or marginalizes large sections of the population, undermines their subsistence security and leads to loss of cultural identity and dignity. Through self-help organizations, people with few resources start to change their conditions of production and consumption at micro-level. The approach is more humane, but therefore also displays all the weaknesses of the human character.

Occasionally for political, economic or practical reasons, the poor may line up with the better-off sections of the population who are sympathetic to their cause and do not misuse their position to determine one-sidedly the rules of the game. The associative sector in a micro-setting (village) is not necessarily market-oriented. Its development may result in a greater proportion of productive activities being directed towards self-sufficiency at household, group or village level, for example in food production (see Chapter 9, the holistic development approach in Thailand).

It may steer the development of the village economy in a different direction by enlarging the scope for village level enterprise (processing and storage of agricultural products, sale of producer and consumer goods, such as in the Brazilian case, discussed in Chapter 7).

Thus self-help organization for economic purposes is not a direct attack on the vestiges of economic and political power. It does not take the bull by the horns. The poor are not in a position to take such a risk. Yet it raises their level of voice and eventually puts them in a better position for a more direct approach, able to press for more fundamental reforms (like land reform, access to fishing grounds, etc.). Self-help groups in Brazil which participated in this study at least, view their economic activities in this political perspective.

In political terms, self-help promotion can also be regarded as a deliberate effort to democratize the economic sector. The organizations which emerge in the course of the process, ideally are 'of the people, by the people, for the people' and with their growing impact on the local economy gradually transform its social and economic structure. It starts off from a different type of logic: that of partnership rather than competition. Such a utopian scenario for societal change, of course, cannot be realized in full but only to a certain degree, depending on the extent to which SHOs are capable of overcoming their own inherent weaknesses and coping with negative influences emanating from their immediate environment. SHOs are found to suffer from factionalism and internal rivalries, from domination by a self-interested, sometimes corrupt leadership or management, from lack of solidarity among members, from short-sighted, inefficient management, etc.– all issues to which the SHPIs which participated in this study have had to address themselves, and which they have tried to influence positively.

The associative economy, a definition
The associative sector is a complex of self-help organizations and their
coordinating or federative bodies which together constitute a distinct sector of the
economy, different from the conventional, profit-oriented private sector as well as
from the government-controlled public sector. Associative sector organizations/
enterprises and their membership normally interact commercially with
organizations/enterprises belonging to the other two sectors and as such are an
integral part of the economic system.

The pseudo-cooperative: an unsuccessful intersectoral hybrid

Finally, for a good understanding of our subject of study it might be important to
distinguish the self-help organization – in which the self-help element is clearly
recognizable – from that widespread phenomenon in developing countries which
could be called the 'pseudo-cooperative'. The pseudo-cooperative has the formal
characteristics of a cooperative society, such as formal registration, by-laws, etc.,
but not, or to a very limited extent, the material characteristics such as
organizational autonomy and member participation in decisionmaking processes.
'De jure' it belongs to the associative sector, but 'de facto' it operates rather as a
public sector enterprise controlled by government and used as an integral part of
its 'delivery mechanism' of services to the rural populace.
Such organizations are the expression of the vaulting ambitions of governments
to bring the rural folk into the mainstream of economic development, and not of
the people's rising awareness of their economic reality and their felt need to
change the prevailing economic system by self-help organization and action.
The gradual transformation of this type of official service organization into a
more genuine type of cooperative – a process called 'de-officialization' in
international circles – is still advocated by many protagonists of cooperative
enterprise, but the feasibility of such a scenario is a different matter and not the
concern of this report. However, the reverse is not true: not all formally
registered cooperatives are 'fake' cooperatives dominated by government. The
official cooperative sector also counts some impressive success stories which are
documented by COPAC in its more recent publications and which show
governments to have played sometimes an important supportive role (COPAC,
1984). In general, however, it seems safe to say that in situations where
government departments have had the upper hand, sometimes even monopolized,
the promotion of cooperative development, the pseudo-cooperative is the rule
and cooperative self-reliance the exception. This has caused the more genuine
types of cooperative organizations in need of a legal status to opt for a 'different
type' of statute. Such an option has also been taken by the SHOs whose
performance is reviewed in this study. The Brazilian APAEB is registered as an
'association', the Indonesian UBs operate as 'pre-cooperatives' and the Thai
SHOs just as 'groups'. The Brazilian situation is different insofar that, where 'de-
officialization' has been effected the cooperatives have often been taken over by a
small elite of big farmers, a situation comparable with the cooperative
development history in some states of India.
The official cooperative sector does not stand alone in its frequent violation of
the principles which it claims to defend and practise. At a time when nearly all
rural development programmes and projects claim to stand for 'people's

20

participation', we often see the concept reduced to a point where it becomes merely a means of manipulating the people's decision-making.

NGOs as self-help promotion institutions

The rural poor, being trapped in a vicious circle of self-perpetuating and self-reinforcing poverty, need some support from outsiders who assist them in finding ways and means to pool their resources, identify viable, gainful and meaningful economic activities, develop systems of accountable leadership and management, manage funds, keep records of income and expenditure, etc. Whereas small entrepreneurs belonging to the rural elite may not need technical and financial assistance or moral support, or only to a lesser extent, the rural poor certainly do.*

Development literature is replete with arguments as to why NGOs are in a better position than government agencies to elicit people's participation and buttress grassroot level initiatives; yet the expertise and manpower required for effective self-help promotion, especially in the economic field, are still underestimated. NGOs are often understaffed and short of trained field workers. Sooner or later, high level expertise will be drawn away to other sectors of the economy or government service which offer better career prospects. NGOs are also not immune from the shortcomings normally attributed to government bureaucracies. Some recent evaluation studies of local NGO performance have shown that this does not always meet expectations, especially in the field of income generation (Guéneau, 1985; for an overview of recent studies on NGO development impact see H. v.d. Heijden, OECD, 1985). This is not to deny the unique potential of NGOs in self-help promotion. But rather than taking this potential for granted, their merits and demerits should be carefully considered and assessed, with a view to finding ways and means of improvement. Such an assessment has been undertaken in the present study, but it differs from conventional approaches in that the local NGOs themselves were the chief actors in the assessment process.

Key concepts of self-help promotion defined

Clarity of theoretical concepts is essential to a fruitful discussion on practical matters. The following is an attempt to define the precise content of such concepts which take a central place in the discussion of self-help and its role in reshaping the economic system.

21

*Kilby and D'Zmura's study (1985), conducted for AID, concluded that 'the major development problem for small business is a lack of capital (particularly of working-credit). Technical assistance in contrast (provision of management and technical know-how, etc.) was revealed to be largely insignificant in the promotion of small business in the traditional (informal) sector' (quotation from Osner, 1986b).

Self-help is any voluntary action undertaken by an individual or group of persons which aims at the satisfaction of individual or collective needs or aspirations. The distinctive feature of a self-help initiative or activity is the substantial contribution made from the individual's or group's own resources in terms of labour, capital, land and/or entrepreneurial skills.

Self-help can be concerned with political, economic, social or cultural activities. In this study, however, we are primarily concerned with economic activities and self-help at the group level. This is not to minimize the importance of self-help at the individual, household or farm level, rather it is a logical outflow of the fact that, in order to achieve economies of scale, those with few resources are left with no other choice than to pool their resources and collaborate for their common benefit. Further, only by group effort can those without power develop sufficient bargaining power on the market to influence prices, and sufficient claim-making power with development authorities to influence administrative decision-making. In the Thai case-study, as we shall see, the 'group' concept in the case of some activities is widened to encompass the entire village community, especially when it comes to deciding on a strategy for achieving self-sufficiency at village level in food production and certain other basic necessities.

At supra-village level, the concept of self-help finds its expression in 'movement building', which in this study is dealt with as one of the eight instruments of self-help promotion.

It may be difficult for western minds to conceive that 'self' need not necessarily mean 'me' as an individual; it can also be conceived as 'we' as a group, 'as long as the group is basically egalitarian' (Schrijvers, 1985). Self-help, as a concept, may be difficult to translate into other languages. Among the conceptual problems which have arisen in the course of this study, 'self-help' has turned out to be the most problematic (see further below under Chapter 4, 'Problems encountered').

Economic activities

The concept of economic activities encompasses all those activities undertaken by individuals or groups which are concerned with the production of material goods or services and have economic value. By implication such goods and services are scarce, command a price in the market or, alternatively, can be used directly for the satisfaction of the consumption needs of its producers (income in kind).

Self-help organizations (SHO)

A self-help organization (SHO) denotes the institutional framework for individuals or households who have agreed to cooperate on a continuing basis to pursue one or more objectives.

A self-help organization is a membership organization which implies that its risks, costs and benefits are shared among its members on an equitable basis and that its leadership and/or manager are liable to be called to account by membership for their deeds.

22

Self-help promotion

Self-help promotion is any deliberate effort to facilitate the emergence and foster the functioning of SHOs: in the context of this report, of such SHOs whose membership originates primarily from the poorer sections of rural society and which carry on economic activities. Self-help promotion signifies a broader, more comprehensive approach to development than the narrower project approach.

The project approach has a tendency to fragment development assistance into inconsistent parts. In self-help promotion, identification, planning and implementation of economic activities are embedded in a multi-faceted strategy which is put into practice through the deployment of a series of coherent initiatives and measures, called 'self-help promotion instruments'.
Self-help promotion, thus conceived, can be broken down into a range of interrelated instruments or promotional services which are directed specifically to SHOs and their membership.

Self-help promotion instruments
The eight instruments of self-help promotion identified in the present study are:
– identification of target population and target groups
– identification of economic activities through participatory research and
  planning
– education and mutual training
– resource mobilization (including savings) and resource provision (including
  credit)
– management consultancy
– linkage building with third parties
– process extension and movement building
– monitoring and ongoing self-evaluation (MOE).
The *growing* participation of SHOs and their federative bodies in the administration of the instruments is considered essential in order to avoid manipulation of SHOs and their membership by self-help promotion institutions or other supporting agencies. The eight instruments are further defined and described in Chapter 3.

Self-help promotion institutions (SHPI)
A self-help promotion institution is an organization in a developing country which has been charged with, or has set itself the task of self-help promotion. To achieve this goal the SHPI disposes of a series of instruments. Promotion becomes self-promotion when this task is fulfilled by federative organs of SHOs or by SHOs themselves. None of the SHPIs participating in the study came into this category. In the Brazilian case, however, some of the promotional functions were not carried out by MOC, the local NGO, but by APAEB, a regional association of small farmers which in its turn is supported by MOC.

Self-reliance
Self-help is a means to achieve self-reliance. Self-reliance is a state or condition whereby an individual or group of persons having achieved such a condition no longer depends on the benevolence or assistance of third parties to secure individual or group interests. By implication, a self-reliant group has developed sufficient analytical, productive and organizational capacity to design and implement a strategy which effectively contributes to the betterment of the conditions of life of its membership and the maintenance of its independent status.
Self-reliance should not be confused with autarky. In present society, no group or community can survive as a self-sufficient unit. Interaction with other groups has become as unavoidable as it is indispensable. Self-reliance, however, implies a style of interaction with third parties on the basis of equality (for a further

23

elaboration of the concept, see Verhagen 1984, pp. 21-25). Self-reliance like self-help does not exist in a pure, undiluted form. SHOs or a group of SHOs having attained such a condition, are also capable of assuring their own promotion. The relationship between self-help promotion institutions, self-help promotion instruments, self-help organizations, and self-reliance as a self-propelling process can be illustrated as follows:

Figure 2: Self-help promotion as part of a process

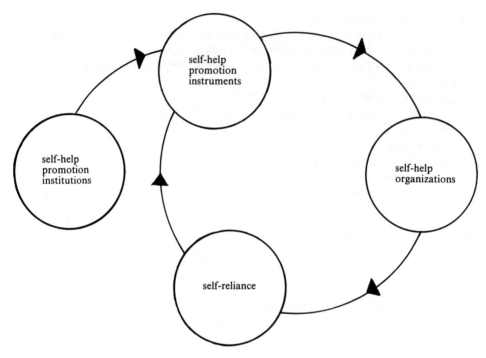

2 The history and objectives of the Cebemo study

History

The inspiration and plan for the undertaking of a study on 'Economic/Rural projects' and 'self-help' emanated from contacts between the German Federal Ministry for Economic Cooperation and Cebemo in the course of 1984 when the German Ministry was in the process of completing a study on 'target group-oriented financing instruments' as a means to promote self-help and combat rural poverty (Osner et al., 1984; DSE, 1985).

One of the conclusions we may draw from the pioneering work of the German Task Force, known as S 24, is that the evaluation of financing instruments is in itself insufficient to develop a suitable concept for the promotion of self-help activities; it needs a larger framework which includes complementary activities such as organization building, training, etc. (Verhagen, 1985, Cebemo Working Document no. 1).

The S 24 Task Force was succeeded by a Special Unit 'Fighting Rural Poverty through self-help', called ES 31, which, in the German Federal Republic, has become an important tool for strengthening NGO-Government collaboration in the specific field of development assistance for self-help promotion. The unit has acted as a catalyst for the further extension of the process at the European level and also in some of the developing countries, by financing joint governmental/non-governmental ventures (Osner, 1986a and 1986b).

Towards the end of 1984, a Cebemo Task Force was set up to prepare and administer a study of its own. The eleven-member Task Force comprised eight participants from Cebemo itself and one each from the Netherlands Ministry of Development Cooperation, the Rabobank (the Netherlands cooperative bank), and the Royal Tropical Institute, Amsterdam. A 'research-coordinator' was appointed in charge of organizing the study and coordinating the field research. The study was given the title 'The promotion of economic activities in rural areas through self-help organizations'. After consultation within the Cebemo organization and with Cebemo partner organizations, the earlier mentioned three organizations in Brazil, Indonesia and Thailand emerged as participant organizations in the study. They commenced and conducted the study during the second half of 1985. Results became available in the course of 1986. The country reports and the preliminary version of the present report were discussed during a two-week consultation which took place in September 1986 in the Netherlands.

In the *selection of participating local NGOs*, the following criteria were used:
– the amount of experience accumulated by the NGO in the promotion of economic activities through SHOs, and the likelihood of its continuing involvement in this particular field of activity;

25

– the willingness and keen interest of the local NGO to collaborate with Cebemo in the undertaking of a participatory study which, unavoidably, would make a claim on the time and energy of its staff;
– the involvement in Cebemo-financed projects as a counterpart organization/project holder;
– the extent to which the NGO was integrated in a network of like-minded local NGOs able to contribute to the research and to benefit from its findings.

Objectives of the study

The following hierarchy of objectives can be distinguished:
1. To facilitate the emancipation of the rural poor, enabling them to achieve a higher degree of socio-economic and intellectual self-reliance.
2. To support the economy of the poor majority by the development of an 'associative economy' (self-help organizations and a system of horizontal and vertical linkages between them) as a means to achieve objective 1.
3. To increase the effectiveness of local NGOs acting as Self-Help Promotion Institutions (SHPIs) in supporting the materialization of objectives 1 and 2.
4. To increase the effectivenes and impact of international assistance, especially of Cebemo as a non-governmental international co-financing agency in supporting the realization of objectives 1 to 3.
5. To gain insight into how the realization of the above objectives could be achieved.
6. To undertake a participatory study which would seek to analyse and assess the strategy, methods of work and performance of a selected number of SHPIs involved in the promotion of economic activities through self-help organizations in rural areas.

Objectives 1 and 2, 'emancipation of the rural poor' and 'development of an associative economy', are development objectives. Objectives 3 and 4, 'increased effectiveness of local NGOs and Cebemo', are organizational objectives which are assumed to be supportive of 1 and 2. Objective 5, 'to gain insight', is a research objective. By means of a participatory study, objective 6, it would be sought to answer the following major research questions:
– What kind of strategy and instruments do the SHPIs (local NGOs) participating in the study use to promote the associative economy among the rural poor? To what extent is the applied instrumentation adequate, sufficiently comprehensive to be effective and consistent with the basic priciples of self-help promotion?
The functioning of SHPIs and their instruments are discussed in Chapters 6 and 8.
– How do the participant SHPIs and SHOs interact with other institutions, governmental and non-governmental, which operate in the same geographical area and also aim at promoting economic activities?
This is discussed in Chapter 6 (pp. 69-71) and Chapter 8 (pp. 115-119).
– What are the structure, functions, organizational and development performance of the self-help organizations (SHOs) promoted by the SHPI concerned?
The performance of SHOs is dealt with in Chapter 7.

– How do external factors (economic, social, political or cultural) impinge upon the type of economic activities undertaken by SHOs, and the choice and use of instruments by the SHPI?

The impact of external factors is discussed by implication when the SHPI activities and SHO performance are reviewed. A separate section of Chapter 9, however, is devoted to a cultural factor, the holistic development perspective in Thailand.

– To what extent are current policies and practices of self-help promotion and self-help activities conditioned and influenced, in a positive or negative way, by the criteria and modes of operation of foreign private co-financing agencies ('donor NGOs')?

The relationship between local SHPIs and foreign funding agencies is considered in Chapter 9, second section.

– In relation to previous questions, what kind of changes or adjustments would be required in objectives, strategies, and functioning of the various institutions constituting the SH promotion system in order to heighten their effectiveness and development performance; changes or adjustments which could also be incorporated in a 3 to 5 year programme of work to be implemented jointly by SHPI and SHOs?

The suggested new orientations are given in Chapter 8, discussing the eight instruments, and Chapter 9, and are summarized in the concluding Chapter 10. The follow-up programmes prepared by the participant SHPIs are not incorporated in the present report (for a summary of these see 'Report of Consultation', Cebemo, 1986a).

3   Methodology

A conceptual framework for self-help promotion

The framework and its rationale

It is not necessary to reinvent the wheel. There exists already a well documented
body of knowledge on which one can draw for the design of a conceptual
framework that synthesizes the essential aspects of SH promotion.* Such a
framework is useful for both researchers and practitioners to guide, systematize,
analyse, and compare promotional practice and experience.

Such a framework can have many configurations. The one presented in Figure 3
has been designed to fit the specific needs of the Cebemo study and gives a
preponderant place to local NGOs as promoters of self-help at grassroots level.
The framework illustrates a self-help promotion system. Its component parts are
organized units which can be divided into the following categories:
– Self-Help Promotion Institutions (SHPIs)
– Self-Help Organizations (SHOs)
– Federations or representative bodies of the SHOs
– Households (small farmers and landless)
– Other 'Supporting Institutions'

The third category, SHO Federations, will merge with the first category, the
SHPI, where the SHOs together have developed towards a structured self-
propelling movement; in other words the federation has become a SHPI.

Interactions between the above mentioned units can be categorized under eight
different headings, called 'instruments'. Such interactions take place in order to
achieve the systems' intermediate objectives and development aims.

The chief development aim of the system, the 'final output', has been defined as
an associative economy 'supporting the economy of the poor majority';
admittedly a rather loose concept which must be qualified according to the
specific context in which SHPIs and SHOs are operating.

The eight instruments mentioned in column 2 of figure 3 together form a
coherent mix of promotional activities. They can be applied by all four categories
of institutions, but are normally coordinated by one SHPI acting as system
manager. Adopting the system's approach implies an acknowledgement of the
interrelationship and interdependence between the above mentioned units. It is a
recognition of the fact that 'economic projects' are implemented in the context of

---

*Among the mass of literature published during the early eighties on participatory approaches and the
self-help type of rural institutions we may mention the synthetic work of FAO Consultation (1982),
Galjart and Buijs (1982), Röling and de Zeeuw (1983), Verhagen (1984), Esman and Uphoff (1984),
DSE (1985).

Figure 3: Key elements of a systematic approach to inducing and sustaining self-help organizations

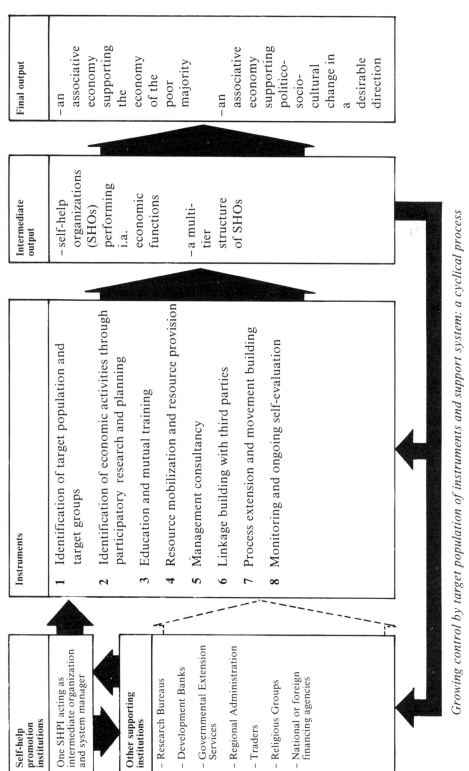

Growing control by target population of instruments and support system: a cyclical process

Final output
– an associative economy supporting the economy of the poor majority
– an associative economy supporting politico-socio-cultural change in a desirable direction

Intermediate output
– self-help organizations (SHOs) performing i.a. economic functions
– a multi-tier structure of SHOs

Instruments	
1	Identification of target population and target groups
2	Identification of economic activities through participatory research and planning
3	Education and mutual training
4	Resource mobilization and resource provision
5	Management consultancy
6	Linkage building with third parties
7	Process extension and movement building
8	Monitoring and ongoing self-evaluation

Self-help promotion institutions
One SHPI acting as intermediate organization and system manager

Other supporting institutions
– Research Bureaus
– Development Banks
– Governmental Extension Services
– Regional Administration
– Traders
– Religious Groups
– National or foreign financing agencies

29

a larger system and that cutting off the analysis at the boundary of a project is counterproductive to gaining good insight and understanding of why things are as they are.

For a better understanding of the framework and the interactions which it is meant to illustrate, some additional comments on SHPIs, 'supporting organizations' and their role, might be helpful.

A Self-Help Promotion Institution (SHPI)
A SHPI is an organization based within the developing country itself: in the Cebemo initiated research, a local NGO with a regional focus covering one or several provinces. In an authentic self-help scenario, a NGO acting as a SHPI will endeavour to *change* from its existing status as an autonomous, independent organization into a representative body owned and controlled by the SHOs. Alternatively, it may seek to make itself redundant by transferring vital promotional functions to secondary or tertiary level institutions which are part and parcel of an autonomous structure of SHOs.* In the Brazilian situation for example, the SHPI MOC has helped to establish a Regional Association of small farmers (APAEB) which de facto functions as a secondary level service-organization.

APAEB not only carries out important economic functions, such as the wholesaling of consumer goods, but it also performs promotional functions in such fields as education, management consultancy and extension of the process to other areas. This points to another distinctive feature of a SH promotion system: SH promotion is not just a matter of promoting grassroots level groups; SHOs eventually should be able to take care of their own promotion. This consideration puts us right at the heart of one of the most critical issues in self-help promotion: *the poor, while they remain poor, cannot afford to pay in full for their own promotion.* Such costs would come as an addition to the costs of maintenance of their own local SHO. In consequence, a SHPI wanting to devote all its time and energy to promoting the rural poor will need special financial resources, local or foreign. Financial self-reliance at SHPI level, therefore, seems to be incompatible with a consistently pursued 'target-group' orientation. In the present study this dilemma – false or true? – is best illustrated by the Indonesian case as discussed in Chapter 6, 'SHPIs in the three countries' compared .

Supporting organizations
By way of illustration, figure 3 mentions in the lower rectangle of the first columm a series of 'supporting organizations' which do not operate under the control of the SHPI or SHOs, yet are considered to form an integral part of the promotion system. Together with the SHPI they constitute *the inter-organizational support structure* which to a large extent conditions the success or failure of the economic activities of SHOs. Their importance varies with the nature and accessibility of the resources they administer such as supply of inputs, know-how, transport facilities, finances, training, etc.

30

* The membership of secondary institutions is made up not of individuals but of primary organizations such as self-help groups or cooperatives. When secondary institutions in their turn form their own federative body, a tertiary level institution is created.

Coordination of activities between the local SHPI/NGO and other institutions intervening in the rural milieu and sometimes aiming at the same target population, proves again and again one of the greatest stumbling blocks in SH promotion. Many of these institutions, in spite of their 'support' potential, in practice show indifference to, or even obstruct self-help promotion. Government departments for example are often found to be suspicious of NGO intervention; established banking institutions may keep a wary eye on the development of independent savings and credit groups; other NGOs operating in the same geographical area carry on their own strategies and practices which may go against the basic principles of self-help promotion. Examples of such counterproductive behaviour are the distribution of interest-free loans to individual farmers or the management of economic activities by NGO staff rather than by SHO members or their representatives.

Not all supporting institutions enter into direct contact with the target population. Most foreign financing agencies deliberately refrain from doing so and restrict their support to financial assistance to the local SHPI/NGO; other regional or national supporting institutions may do the same and use the local NGO/SHPI only as a channel for the disbursement of funds and the distribution of production inputs (seed, fertiliser, etc.).

The network of supporting institutions is normally rather complex and fluid: in the course of time supporters may shift to the opposite camp and vice versa. In this process of shifting alliances between organizations, organizational interests and personal sympathies or rivalries normally play a preponderant role, even if, officially, all claim to give priority concern to the interests of the target population.

It is important to formulate explicitly some of the premises which give the framework its logical basis and rationale of construction. No single organization, Self-Help Promotion Institution (SHPI) or Supporting Institution, can carry the full responsibility for SH promotion and provide the full range of services which emerging Self-Help Organizations (SHOs) may require. Hence the need for inter-organizational collaboration between a SHPI and other local governmental, non-governmental and/or commercial private institutions.

Instruments
It is possible to break down the range of services which SHOs and their membership require into a series of identifiable 'instruments' of SH promotion, such as mentioned in the second column of the chart, i.e. identification of the target population and target groups, participatory research and planning, training, resource provision, etc. The growing control by SHO leadership and members of the instruments and support system is indicated by the arrow running in the reverse direction at the bottom of the chart. The instruments are the subject of detailed discussion later in this chapter.

Self-Help Organizations (SHOs)
Self-Help organizations (SHOs), shown in the third column, are the logical output of SH promotion activities among the rural poor. SHOs are base-level, primary organizations. By themselves they can exercise but little influence on the larger economic and political setting of which they are part. Hence the need for networking and structuring of interactions. Informal networks among SHOs are an important first step towards the gradual build-up of a multi-level or multi-tier

structure of horizontal and vertical linkages which will bring new economic opportunities within the reach of SHOs and their membership.

SHOs are regarded as no more than an 'intermediate output' of the system. What matters is not the institutional product but its final 'output', i.e. the extent to which the development functions and performance of SHOs affect positively the conditions of production and consumption at the household or group level. The emerging associative economy may in its turn contribute to desirable patterns of social, political or cultural change, to the extent that it responds to the aspirations of the rural poor.

Process analysis

A promotion system can be studied at a given moment, but its working can only be properly understood if considered in a historical perspective. The *process analysis*, i.e. how interactions between system elements have evolved in the course of time, is therefore an essential ingredient of any research effort that seeks a deeper understanding of why things are as they are.

SH promotion as represented in Figure 3 is thus conceived as a cyclical process. In the course of time the target population gets increased control over the instruments, thus strengthening the process's self-propelling nature.

External factors

The way a promotional system operates and develops depends not only on its internal dynamics but also on a great variety of external factors. These external, environmental conditions hamper or facilitate the system in its operations and achievement of objectives. They can be divided into economic, politico-administrative, socio-cultural, historical, technological and physico-climatological conditions. Where external conditions obstruct a desirable course of action, they are often referred to as 'constraints'. Two recent studies, however, suggest that environmental constraints are not as crucial to the success or failure of SHOs as is normally assumed in development literature (Esman and Uphoff, 1984; DSE, 1985). The practice of SH promotion shows that SHOs emerge in a wide variety of economic, political and physical conditions. More important than the conditions themselves appears to be how people acting in such an environment react upon them. This is an encouraging finding: it is not the environment that is determinant but 'what people living in those environments choose to do about them' (Esman & Uphoff, 1984, p.126). For example, sex discrimination, a cultural factor, may be a serious constraint on women's participation in self-help organization, but it may also be a stimulus for the formation of women-only self-help organizations, once women have concluded that if they do not help themselves, nobody else will. Self-help normally comes as a response to a challenge. Self-help promotion, as a development strategy, assumes that the rural poor, in addition to this, need some assistance from relative outsiders in a long-term learning process that will enable them to find the appropriate responses to an ever-changing environment.

The Cebemo-initiated research proposed, and this was accepted by the local NGOs, to study the impact of external conditions in a purely inductive way, that is to say on the basis of concrete experiences gained by the NGOs acting as

32

Figure 4: The relationship of the SHPI/SHO complex to its environment

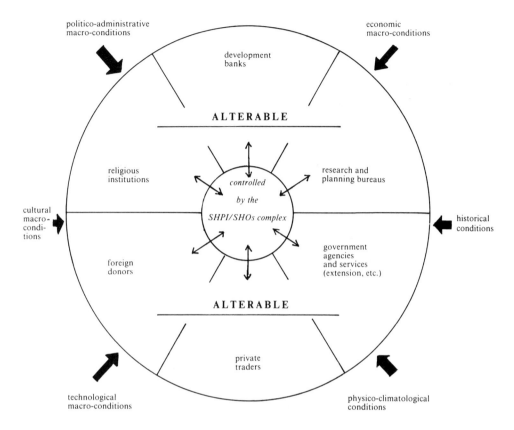

SHPIs, and by the SHOs in the pursuit of their economic, social and political objectives.

From the perspective of the SHPI/SHO complex (the SHOs together with their ally the SHPI) we can distinguish three levels of environment, using as the main criterion the extent to which it can be controlled and influenced. The levels are visualized in Figure 4.* They are:

33

* Design adjusted from World Bank (1980), pp. 11-12.

– The internal environment of the SHPI/SHO complex, which corresponds to the innermost circle on the chart. The SHPI/SHO complex in fact is a sub-system within the larger SH promotion system. The larger system includes the 'Supporting Organizations'.

Within their sub-system the SHPI and SHOs are the masters, who give shape to their mutual relationship and interactions and decide on how to react to the impulses which come from the external environment. But who, within the SHPI/ SHO sub-system, the actual masters are, is a different matter.

– The second level is that of the SH promotion system, which we discussed earlier in this chapter. As stated, the 'supporting institutions' are part of it. SHPI staff and SHO leaders endeavour to influence the policies and practices of the supporting institutions with a view to making them more effective in attaining the SHPI and SHO objectives. SHPI and SHOs in their turn are influenced by the policies and practices of these institutions. Where the relationship tends to be more co-operative than competitive, supporting institutions can be regarded as part of the system. This part of the SHPI/SHOs environment can be regarded as 'alterable'. The arrows between the inner circle (the SHPI/SHO sub-system) and the outer circle (the SH promotion system) therefore go in a two-way direction.

– The third level is situated beyond the boundaries of the SH promotion system. These are the macro-conditions which cannot be altered by the combined or individual action of a SHPI or SHO. The country's political system, rate of inflation, patterns of income distribution, sex discrimination, population growth, religious beliefs, etc. make up the setting of the SH promotion system and must be considered as its 'givens'. The arrows emerging from the outer system therefore go in one direction, which is a recognition of their impact on the SH promotion system as a whole and the need for an appropriate response.

Finally it is important to realize that boundaries of influence are not fixed once and for all. Where a SH movement gains in economic strength, its manipulative power also increases. Decisions formerly taken unilaterally within the external system become negotiable and alterable when the target population becomes well organized and is effectively supported by a SHPI. New and more complex economic activities become possible, such as wholesale marketing, processing of produce etc., when SHOs federate in larger units, and this also augments their claim-making powers vis-à-vis third parties, including government. It is exactly by widening its boundaries that a SH movement can overcome some of its limiting economic and political conditions, can increase the chances of its continued existence, and become a factor of change in macro-processes.

A conceptualization of the performance of Self-Help Organizations

In Chapter 7 we shall assess the performance of SHOs promoted by the SHPIs in the three countries.

In considering SHO performance, it is convenient to distinguish between organizational performance and development performance.

In discussing *organizational performance* we shall deal with the extent to which SHOs have been able to concretize the self-help concept and move towards self-reliance in terms of:

– *administrative autonomy* defined as the capacity of leaders and members to determine and decide by themselves on the long and short term objectives of their organizations and the direction to follow, to achieve such objectives;

– *managerial autonomy* defined as the capacity to manage by themselves day-to-day operations;
– *financial autonomy*, which refers to the SHO's ability to stand on its own feet financially and be independent of financial assistance from third parties for ensuring continuity of activities.

In relation to each of the three above mentioned aspects of self-reliance we shall consider the extent to which, and how, SHO members participate in the decision-making process (contribute to administrative autonomy), in the management and implementation of activities (contribute to managerial autonomy), and in the mobilization of financial resources (contribute to financial autonomy).

When assessing the SHOs *development performance* we shall differentiate between economic, social, political and cultural impact.

The impact element in the study was given greater emphasis than originally conceived in the Cebemo design, because it was the general feeling of the action-researchers in the three countries that this study should also serve to deepen their insight into the dynamics of the economy of the poor, their feelings and aspirations, and how these relate to the ongoing economic activities of the SHOs, promoted by the SHPI. This ambitious research objective, as we shall see later, could be realized in part only. Yet it was a worthwhile and essential complement to the other research activities. In particular, the dialogues at household level revealed important knowledge gaps on the part of SHPI staff concerning the economy of the poor, and heightened the action-researchers' awareness of the interrelationship between the economic and socio-cultural dimensions of self-help action and organization.

Concerning impact the study looked at the following dimensions:
– *economic*, which deals with the impact of micro-projects on production, distribution and consumption of goods and services;
– *social*, which deals with matters of social concern, social justice, responsible behaviour;
– *political*, which, in the context of the present research, deals with the distribution of power at group and village level, and the capacity to influence decisions at supra-village level as a result of group formation;
– *cultural*, which, for the present research, deals primarily with changes in the value-system and their expression in the economic, social and political spheres of life.

Changes in the four above mentioned fields are analysed as follows:
– at individual or household level (impact on men and women may differ);
– at group or SHO level;
– at village level;
– beyond village level, especially where SHOs from different villages collaborate.

The basic questions to be investigated in respect of each 'micro-project' promoted directly or indirectly by the SHPI were the following:
– Have the economic, social, or political conditions of the target population, and the related value-system, changed in significant ways as a result of SHO economic activities?
– If so, in what direction?
– To what extent? and
– How is the choice of such activities and their impact related to the promotional practices of the SHPI?

From an excursion into the theory and practice of impact assessment it was learnt that so far there seems to be very little experimentation with approaches which involve the so-called 'beneficiaries' in the development of indices of positive and negative impact, let alone the integration of such indices into an ongoing monitoring and evaluation system. Conventional approaches to impact assessment or 'measurement' can only be of limited relevance to SH promotion because they respond to criteria of success established by the international or national development administrations and implicitly deny the capacity of judgement and the priorities of the main development actors (= 'target population') themselves.*

The attempted assessment of development performance can be seen as the synthesis of three streams of information and mental processes:
– a re-interpretation of factual findings on SHPI and SHO activities;
– the exchange of ideas with SHO leaders and membership on what they consider as the more direct effects and impact of SHO activities on their situation;
– in the Brazilian and Indonesian cases, the information collected from a small number of households in the research villages on household income and expenditure.
What could be done within the framework of the present study was no more than an approximation of direct effects and impact. Precise measurement, if possible at all, was not the purpose.

Eight self-help promotion instruments

In the original design of the study, it was hypothesized that there are eight categories of variables which in many circumstances have a decisive impact on the emergence, functioning and development performance of SHOs. They have been termed *instruments* because they correspond to identifiable, operational tasks in the field and are to a large extent under the control of the system's actors. They can also be referred to as the 'internal factors' of the SH promotion system as distinct from the external factors which we discussed earlier in this chapter. These internal factors are referred to in development literature as 'conditions of success', most recently in the earlier mentioned CEC Evaluation Study (Crombrugge et al., 1985). The present study was not so much concerned with the reaffirmation of this part of development theory but with the more practical concern of how to operationalize such interrelated concepts as participatory planning, resource mobilization, leadership development, etc., in the field situation. It also tried to assess the causes and consequences of a particular instrument not being applied at all or in a manner not consistent with self-help promotion. In this study, the use of the term 'conditions' has been restricted to external conditions. As to internal factors, i.e. the mechanisms at the programme/project level which lend themselves to management, 'instruments' was considered a more appropriate term than 'conditions'.

36

* A clear exception to this general statement is the FAO publication *Guiding principles for People's Participation Projects*, 1983 by Gerrit Huizer.

SH promotion, so it has been assumed, works through a carefully selected combination of instruments, which are applied simultaneously once the process has started, although the exact combination depends on the stage of development and local conditions. Acceptance of the system's idea implies recognition that the whole is more than a simple addition of its constituent parts, in other words, that participatory planning alone, or savings and credit alone, or training alone, cannot do the job, and are in themselves insufficient for eliciting a self-sustaining process of self-help action and organization among the rural poor. SH promotion as represented in Figure 3 is also a cyclical process with the target population acquiring increased control over the instruments, thus strengthening the process' self-propelling nature.

If, in this study, for analytical reasons, we treat the instruments as distinct from each other, this is not to minimize their interrelationship. For example a good project 'evaluation' session in a village may shed new light on the economy of the poor ('participatory analysis'), have a high intrinsic educational value ('education') and serve the purpose of 'process extension' where persons from neighbouring villages have had the opportunity to participate. In fact we should be aware that in self-help promotion, specific promotional activities with a prime focus on target group identification, or planning, or training, or savings mobilization, etc., are likely to cross the boundaries of categorization when applied with a high degree of consistency to each other. Nevertheless, in view of the importance of each of them as part of a comprehensive development approach, they merit separate analysis and discussion. The following short definitions and descriptions may be helpful:

Instrument 1: Identification of target population and target groups
This is the process through which the rural poor, as groups or as individuals, are identified, or encouraged to identify themselves, as potential partners in development. Identification takes place on the basis of criteria which are specific to the area or location, and are determined from the perspective of the rural population itself. Criteria may refer to ownership of assets, such as land or livestock, or access to other income generating activities; or to living conditions such as housing. Where the rural poor are already organized in groups, the identification process may relate to groups rather than to individuals. Identification of target population or groups may be undertaken by the SHPI in interaction with local key-informants, including the rural poor themselves. The identification process may also run in the opposite direction when local groups on their own initiative contact an existing SHPI. From the case-studies we shall see that 'identification' is normally a two-way process with the SHPI performing a more active or passive role depending on circumstances. From a self-help perspective, a more suitable wording of the concept might be 'mutual identification of development actors and their promoters'.

Instrument 2: Participatory research and planning   37
Participatory research refers to the active participation of the target population and groups in diagnostic and problem-solving thinking about development constraints and their present socio-economic position. Its aim is to identify economic activities through which they could overcome such constraints and thus improve their position. Participatory planning is the logical extension of participatory research and implies the target population's participation in the assessment of the feasibility of the proposed action and in the planning of

operations. The feasibility assessment comprises several dimensions: economic, social, political, technical and operational.

Instrument 3: Education and mutual training
In common usage education and training denote essentially a one-way transmission of standardized packages of knowledge and skills from educated to non-educated, from skilled to unskilled. Against this, in self-help promotion, education and training refer to a synthesis of expertise brought in from outside and the experiential knowledge of the rural poor. The result of this process is new knowledge which is well adjusted to the local situation. Education and training in this conception are the purposeful creation of a learning situation which leaves ample room for the two-way communication of ideas and the transfer of skills. Because of their connotation with top-down forms of intervention the terms 'education and training' might be considered inappropriate to indicate such a process and replaced by 'knowledge sharing and knowledge generation'.

Instrument 4: Resource mobilization and resource provision
Resource mobilization is used to denote the process of pooling and putting to practical use the productive resources owned or possessed by (potential) members of SHOs. Resources can be natural (land, water), financial (money), material (seeds, grains, manure) or non-material (know-how, entrepreneurial skills, claim-making or bargaining power). Through pooling of resources the poor achieve economies of scale and levels of knowledge or influence which are beyond the reach of the individual.
Resource provision refers to the acquisition of additional financial or material resources from external sources (credit, productive inputs). In self-help promotion external resource provision is complementary to the contributions members of SHOs are able to make from their own resources. The question is how far resource provision should and can go to enable the poor to break through the vicious circle of self-perpetuating poverty without destroying or undermining their self-help potential, as often happens in cases of outside assistance.

Instrument 5: Management consultancy
Management consultancy denotes the assistance given in terms of advice with a view to ensuring the efficient use of resources by local SHOs or their higher level organizations, and in a direction consistent with the objectives of the organization. Consultancy can address itself to different aspects of management which are central to SHO performance and continuity. It includes:
– the management of financial resources, *financial management*;
– the management of human resources (labour), of productive assets (equipment, buildings) and of natural resources (land, water); these tasks, together, can be denoted as *organizational management*;
– the management of conflicts; conflicts invariably arise in any organization between groups or between persons who have to work together, while pursuing different personal or organizational objectives; this can be referred to as *conflict management*;
– *technical management* which is directly related to the technology used by the SHO.
Management consultancy as a SH promotion instrument assumes that even when economic activities have been well prepared and planned, new and unforeseen

financial, economic, operational and technical problems will emerge in the course of action, for which the SHO may need some outside advice and/or assistance. Management consultancy can be viewed as a special, non-material form of resource provision and as such it carries the danger of imposition of ideas by the adviser on the SHO, leading to a feeling of inadequacy among SHO leaders and membership. Even so, there seems to be general agreement that management consultancy is a legitimate need of any productive organization, which must be gratified, provided that it does not shift the responsibility for decision-making and management from leaders and staff to their advisers.

Instrument 6: Linkage building with third parties
Conceptually we can distinguish:
– linkage building within the narrow SHPI/SHO sub-system or SH movement, to be discussed in the next section under instrument 7, and
– linkage building within the larger system of SH promotion, i.e. linkage building with third parties such as government agencies, private banks, traders, etc.
Linkage-building with third parties denotes the build-up of a network of linkages between, on the one hand, the SHPI/SHO sub-system, and on the other, various administrative or economic units whose support, service, collaboration or tolerance are necessary for the smooth functioning of the SHOs.
In recent years, there has been a great deal of interest in the relationship between governmental and non-governmental organizations. The relationship is often referred to as one of mutual suspicion and tension but capable of improvement. But also in other spheres of activity, the relationship between the SHPI/SHO complex and third parties such as private industry, traders, banks, religious institutions, is rather complex and varied. The process of linkage building with third parties is of a dialectical nature and as such its evolution also includes the severance or reduction of existing linkages which are no longer considered functional or are found to be counter-productive.

Instrument 7: Process extension and movement building
By *process extension* is meant the extension of self-help activities and self-help organizations over wider geographical areas as a process which gradually covers a larger segment of the underprivileged strata of society.
Movement building is defined as the process of structuring the relationship between SHOs and the SHPI, and in particular between SHOs, both vertically and horizontally, into a multi-tier pyramid-shaped structure.
SH promotion implies a deliberate attempt to facilitate and speed up these two processes.
In process extension the main issue is how a process, once successfully started in a few places, e.g. villages, can spread to other places without a proportionate increase in costs of promotion, viz. number of project staff, costs of transport, etc. One strategy often practised to keep costs of process extension low and make it more effective, is the involvement of local leaders who dispose of persuasive and motivating powers which normally exceed those of professional field staff.
Movement building implies the development of a network, both horizontally and vertically, between SHOs and their higher level organizations. At the same time it is evident that SHOs, unless they work together in at least a second level structure, will not be able to undertake more complex types of economic activities which require a larger scale of operation. But experience has also shown that the advantages of vertical organization are not automatic. The Brazilian case study is

one of many to show that when a structure becomes more complex, it may easily lead to the domination by higher tier organizations over affiliated lower level organizations and to decreased commitment and loyalty on the part of the membership (see Chapter 8). Academics and practitioners both agree on the need for linkages between primary level organizations ('networking') without which they cannot be expected to have more than a relatively small impact on the larger economic and social world. The most appropriate shape of the linkage system, more vertical or more horizontal, and the distribution of administrative and economic functions between the different levels, are issues in an ongoing debate between organizations which form part of a multi-tier structure.

Instrument 8: Monitoring and ongoing self-evaluation
Monitoring, as part of a SH promotion system, can be defined as the periodic review by development actors and promoters of ongoing activities at every level of the system, and the assessment of whether or not activities are proceeding efficiently according to operational plans, and reaching their specific objectives. Ongoing self-evaluation is a process whereby the development actors and their promoters determine systematically the relevance, effectiveness and impact of activities undertaken at every level of the SH promotion system, in the light of its long-term development objectives. It is 'viewed as a dialogue over time and not as a static picture at one point of time' (Porter and Clark, 1985).
The difference between monitoring and ongoing self-evaluation resides mainly in the time perspective from which the assessment takes place: the first, monitoring, is closely related to ongoing concrete activities; the second, evaluation, implies an overarching reflection on the development relevance and significance of the self-help activities and related promotional practice.
Monitoring and evaluation are widely accepted as valid components of programme or project organization. However, in a conventional approach they are organized as separate activities entrusted to special staff or outsiders who can assess progress and performance objectively and in a detached manner. In a participatory approach, monitoring and evaluation activities are integrated in the working tasks of field workers, leaders of SHOs and other development agents, while special efforts are made to involve the target population itself (the development actors) in the process. The emphasis is thus on self-evaluation. Experience shows that executive staff of SHPIs and SHOs are often so overwhelmed by operational tasks that systematic and regular assessment of strategy, working methods and performance does not take place unless such a process is organized and receives the recognition and status of a useful instrument. In fact, indications of the absence of such a mechanism provided part of the rationale for this study and for organizing it as a self-evaluation exercise by the Cebemo partner organizations.
It might be convenient to distinguish three levels where monitoring and self-evaluation may need special organizational effort:
40
– At the micro-level, i.e. at the level of primary organizations (= base-level SHOs). This implies the assessment by SHO members themselves and their leaders of the effectiveness of the instruments in relation to the functioning of their own organizations.
– At the level of the SHPI, primarily among SHPI staff.
– At the level of the SH promotion system which assumes participation by delegates from 'other supporting institutions'.

The degree of participation by the target population in MOE activities will very much depend on how the process is organized and where evaluation meetings are held (in the field or in town offices).

Nature and scope of study

The study in each of the three countries is:
- action-based,
- participatory,
- programme preparatory and
- multi-level.

By *'action-based'* is meant that the research capitalizes on concrete and mostly ongoing experiences with 'economic projects' in which self-help is the central issue. In most cases, these were made possible through donor funding.

By *'participatory'* is meant the active participation of the SHPI staff (local NGO) and the members and leaders of SHOs in the analytical process. As to the latter category it is assumed that the perceptions and opinions held at the grassroots about development constraints and the effectiveness and impact of ongoing economic activities have scientific value and should be incorporated in the research process.

By *'programme preparatory'* is meant that the research will be helpful in the formulation and determination of a medium-term development programme to be implemented by the participant SHPI and collaborating SHOs. This 'voltar a pratica' (Brazilian report, p. 9), 'returning to practice' of whatever the study has yielded in terms of insights into more effective approaches to SH promotion, was facilitated by the fact that most of the research team members are also practitioners.

The *'multi-level'* nature of the study is illustrated by figure 5, which distinguishes four levels of development action: the household, the village, the regional and international levels. The SHPIs which have participated in the present study operate at regional level. For this reason the national level has been omitted in figure 5.

The foci of research are indicated in figure 5 in capital letters or bold. They are 'SHOs', 'INSTRUMENTS' (= the interface between SHOs and SHPIs) and further 'Local NGOs' or 'Federation of SHOs, acting as a SHPI'. In small characters are given the 'households' because only a small number of households were covered by the study through in-depth investigations. Their 'interaction' with the self-help groups/organizations was studied at less depth than originally intended, as were the operations of 'supporting institutions' and their interrelationship. Implications of the study for the relationship between the foreign private co-financing agencies and the local NGOs were analysed mainly from the perspective of the participant local NGOs.

41

Coverage
Because of the wide scope of the study in terms of the number of variables and their interrelationship, it was hypothesized that a study at greater depth covering only a few localities, SHOs and households within the area of operation of each

*Figure 5: A multi-level approach**

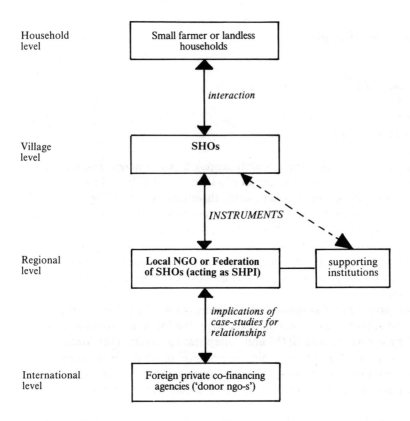

Household
level — Small farmer or landless households

interaction

Village
level — SHOs

INSTRUMENTS

Regional
level — Local NGO or Federation of SHOs (acting as SHPI) — supporting institutions

implications of case-studies for relationships

International
level — Foreign private co-financing agencies ('donor ngo-s')

*Foci of research in capital letters or bold

SHPI, was preferable to a global survey covering a larger number of SHOs and household units. It was realized that this would reduce the 'external validity' of the findings but it was an unavoidable consequence of the participatory nature of the study.

Figure 6 gives a schematic presentation of the coverage of the organizational units whose functioning was analysed in relation to each other, supporting organizations not included.

The figure illustrates:

– *full* coverage of the local NGOs, acting as SHPIs and participating in the study: in Thailand they were two (the two DISACs), in Indonesia one (Bina Swadaya), and in Brazil also one (MOC);

– coverage by direct investigation of *a sample* of SHOs promoted by the SHPI. All of them, in total twenty, are located in villages in the selected research areas: in Thailand eleven SHOs in two villages; in Indonesia seven spread over two village-clusters; and in Brazil two SHOs based in the research village, one regional federal type of organization (APAEB), and for the economic part of the analysis two more primary units (branches) affiliated to APAEB;

– coverage of only *a tiny section* of total households by the household surveys: the investigations and dialogues at household level were restricted to five to six households per research village or village cluster.

The research was a combination of qualitative and quantitative inquiry with emphasis on the qualitative aspects. The qualitative part of the study focussed on methods of work of the SHPI, issues of leadership and member participation, and the social, political and cultural aspects of self-help promotion.

Quantitative, 'hard-nosed' data, for example, were collected on the economic functioning and financial performance of SHOs, on the income and expenditure of rural households and the effect of the economic activities carried on by the SHOs on the household economy. The local NGO/SHPI was studied, or rather studied itself, in all its structural and functional aspects. Where a SHPI had taken the form of a federative type of organization (Brazil), its financial performance

Figure 6: Schematic presentation of the coverage of units of analysis

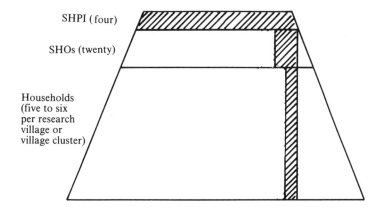

SHPI (four)

SHOs (twenty)

Households
(five to six
per research
village or
village cluster)

was also assessed. The check on representativity, validity and relevance of findings took place through group discussions at village level in workshops with leaders of other SHOs from neighbouring villages, and in workshops at regional or national level with fieldworkers. To these workshops were also invited representatives from other NGOs working in the same professional field or geographical area. The findings of the study concerning SHO performance, impact, and SHO-SHPI relationships are thus primarily based on the processes analysed in a few places, termed 'research villages' or 'research village clusters'. However, during workshops and discussions with fieldworkers and leaders from other areas and locations, participants clearly indicated that to the best of their knowledge the situation elsewhere was not fundamentally different from the one found in the selected research areas and villages.

At this stage of the argument it is important to refer to the relationship between the methodology applied under the present study, and the plea for a departure from conventional technocratically-inspired development thinking as set out in Chapter 1. When a participatory type of development is pursued, inspired by a philosophy that people ought to become the subject rather than the object of development, then this also has consequences for research methods and techniques. In the present study this is reflected in the following orientations:
– making use of the analytical capabilities of non-researchers in the research process, such as SHO members, leaders, field workers;
– faith in the idea that the pooling of ideas between people acting at different levels and judging from different horizons will make for findings of higher relevance and practicability than conventional studies would be able to do;
– recognition that action research is not free of consequences; action-researchers have a moral obligation towards SHO members and leaders who have participated in the study to facilitate appropriate follow-up action during and after the study period.

Lists of items and questions
In the later sections of this book (especially Chapters 5 and 7) we shall see that within the broad framework sketched above, different emphases have been given in each of the three countries as to the scope and depth of study. This has heightened the relevance of the study for the local NGO/SHPI concerned but lessened the comparability of findings between countries. Except for such differences in emphasis we may say that the concepts and conceptual framework, as discussed in the previous sections, have been commonly applied to the three research-sites. Further detailed research questions based on this framework were formulated, and then adjusted and reworded to suit local conditions. Questions and schedules related to:
– History, objectives, structure and functions of SHPIs;
– Items of information on the selected areas and villages;

44

– History, objectives, structure, functions, organizational and development performance of SHOs and impact assessment;
– Items for socio-economic investigation at household level;
– The eight instruments of self-help promotion and the impact of external factors on their use;
– The functioning of the SH promotion system as a whole.
The above lists of items and questions were used as flexible guides. It was left to

the action-researchers' discretion to add items and questions which they felt worth including, or to delete those considered of no relevance.

Sources of information
Sources of information were diverse and included:
– Participant observation during village ceremonies and festivities;
– Group interviewing in the research village at SHO level;
– Listening in when groups held their regular meetings, and informal talks with village inhabitants;
– In-depth investigation of a small sample of households, member as well as non-member: the action-researchers used a framework of topics to be covered, but interviewees (female or male adults) were encouraged to raise other topics as well;
– Documentary sources available at SHPI and SHO level (statistical data, annual accounts) and official documents available with the village head or governmental offices at area level;
– Semi-structured, open-ended interviews with key-informants at village level, and SHPI staff and field staff of other supporting institutions.
During the interviews and group discussions there was no use of fixed or multiple choice questionnaires. Villagers raised new questions, sometimes of greater relevance than those anticipated by the action-researchers (Brazilian report, p. 9). Given the paucity of well-established theory about the interrelationship between the system elements – that complex of institutions and instruments which together form a SH promotion system – the study was exploratory in many respects. Socio-economic emancipation of the poor, self-help and self-help promotion form an interactive, cyclical process. How these three phenomena interrelate and can mutually reinforce each other is extraordinarily contextual. The validity of the conclusions depends primarily on the capacity for integrative thinking and analysis of the research participants. There is, to the writer's knowledge, no generally agreed standard canon for establishing the validity and accuracy of findings of a process in which participants at different levels influence the content and direction of each other's thinking and in which the subjects and objects of study tend to merge into one entity.

Composition of action-research teams

The composition of the three teams of action-researchers shows a mixture of full-timers and part-timers. Some of the team members belong to the regular staff of the participant local NGO; others were especially contracted for the study under the responsibility of the same. Participation by the NGO's own staff was considered essential to ensure relevance and practicability of findings, and interest in follow-up action. Participation by outsiders was necessary as well as desirable, first to strengthen the research capacity of the SHPI, secondly as a correction to possible bias and lack of objectivity in the interpretation of study findings.

The MOC team in *Brazil* comprised four members. All were male and part-timers. They represented a wide array of disciplines such as geology, sociology, and theology. Their need for support in conducting the economic analysis became apparent after the first draft texts had been written. Subsequently this support was provided on an adhoc basis by an economist based at CERIS, Rio de Janeiro, who has fulfilled the additional task of monitoring the progress of work throughout the entire research period. Other MOC field staff participated occasionally in the collection of data at village level and the selection of households for interviewing.

The hard core of the CCTD six-member research team in *Thailand* consisted of two university based social scientists, one male and one female. The university researchers emphasized in their report the importance and indispensability of participation by SHPI staff in the research process, in this particular case of the field workers and directors attached to the two regional centres, viz. the DISACs of Chiengmai and Ubon which de facto operate as SHPIs in their respective regions. The Bangkok based umbrella organization, CCTD, provided the organizational and moral back-up in a somewhat similar role to that played by CERIS in Brazil.

At the centre of the Bina Swadaya team (*Indonesia*) were three persons, one so-called 'integrated expert', based at the Yogyakarta BS field office who was assisted by two Indonesian researchers, one female from another Yogyakarta based NGO and one male BS field worker. Back-up was received from the entire staff attached to the Yogyakarta BS field office (five persons), and from a young Indonesian free-lance university graduate, presently employed by BS. The Jakarta based head of the BS Field Department (PUSBINUB) also acted as the study's supervisor.

The composition of the teams was somewhat problematic in all three countries. In Brazil there was the already mentioned absence of an economist in the initial stages of the study as well as the male dominance within the study team. In Indonesia a preponderant role had to be played by its expatriate member, since the professional local researchers, attached to the Bina Swadaya Jakarta office, were already fully occupied with contract research for other organizations. In all three countries it proved hard to find researchers who were action-research minded, familiar with NGO working styles, and had sufficient time available to direct a study of this nature.

The problems encountered in the organization of the action-research team had a deeper cause common to all the participating NGOs, namely the absence within such organizations of self-evaluation as a regularly undertaken and systematically organized practice (see also Crombrugge et al., 1985). This is a direct outflow of the international system of 'project financing', which in its present form was hypothesized as largely inappropriate for self-help promotion (Chapter 1) and which will be the subject of further scrutiny on the basis of the three country cases in Chapter 9.

46   A plan of operation in ten phases

The study's plan of operation in the three research-sites/countries received its inspiration and orientation from the conceptual framework, the objectives of study and the methodological guidelines set out in the previous chapters. Excluding the preparation phase of the study at Cebemo level, ten major phases can be distinguished although in practice there was much backward and forward movement from one phase to another. Conclusions emerging from one phase were verified in the following and later phases in a different research setting and required short excursions back to earlier phases. Participatory research should be conceived as an iterative, not a linear process; the partial accomplishment of one phase leads to a reshaping of perspectives and instrumentation for the next phase. The analysis is ongoing and not restricted to the final stages of study. The process of analysis thus follows the same logic as the kind of programmes it aims to serve.

Yet if the analytical process is to take an orderly course, there is also a need for structuring it. The way this has been done is recapitulated in Figure 7 and shortly commented upon below.

As to phase 1, the main criterion for the selection of research areas and villages was the level of economic activities undertaken by the local SHOs promoted by the SHPI. The magnitude of the research tasks ahead and the time and manpower limitations (three to four persons, most on a part-time basis over five to six months) were such that within the areas of operation of the participant SHPIs/NGOs, relatively small areas had to be selected and within these only a few localities (villages).

Figure 7: Ten phases of the study's plan of work

location of activity	phases	
developing country	phase 1:	Preparation of the study: Review of conceptual framework and research questions by local NGO. Selection of research sites (province, district and villages) and composition of study team.
area (e.g. district or province)	phase 2:	Review of structure and functions of own organization (SHPI = local NGO) and other supporting institutions operating in the selected research area.
village level mainly	phase 3:	Study of selected self-help organizations, especially their economic activities, participatory household surveys and impact study in selected research localities.
village level	phase 4:	Study of the working and effectiveness of self-help promotion instruments at local level, as applied by the SHPI and other institutions reviewed under phase 2.
intervillage level	phase 5:	Extension of study to other localities to test relevance of findings to wider geographical area.
area level	phase 6:	Study of relevance of findings and the effectiveness of the self-help promotion system continued at the level of SHPI and other supporting institutions consulted in phase 2.
developing country	phase 7:	Preparation of preliminary version of country-specific research reports (Brazil, Thailand, Indonesia).
	phase 8:	Participatory Workshop at SHPI level with field workers, SHO delegates and supporting institutions' representatives.
	phase 9:	Drafting of final version of country reports and follow-up programme.
The Netherlands	phase 10:	Preparation of preliminary version of 'integrated report'. Consultation of policy makers and study teams of the three participant SHPIs (NGOs) and Cebemo. Preparation of final report.

47

During phases two to six field research was conducted at the meso and micro level involving prolonged stays within the research villages. Each phase corresponded to specific research questions to be answered, and had its specific set of research instruments which were tested out and constantly adjusted. The number of households studied at village level was kept small, on average six per village, giving preference to depth of study and dialogue rather than number of households covered, and also to informal group discussions and talks with key informants rather than formal interviewing. Concerning the economic performance of SHOs, special attention was given to financial and managerial autonomy and to 'hidden subsidies' which might cause prolonged dependence of SHOs on SHPI assistance.

Through discussions and workshops at the various levels, viz. group, village, inter-village, area and national level, and finally through a consultation between participant SHPIs and Cebemo at international level, an attempt was made to draw the maximum number of persons and experiences into the analytical process. Such consultations at various levels also laid the groundwork for willing cooperation in the design and implementation of follow-up activities.

Limitations of the study

The present study has certain limitations with respect to generalizability of findings and possible bias in the process of interpretation of data. These are a direct outflow of the organization of the study as predominantly selfevaluative and qualitative in nature, giving priority to depth over representativity at practically all phases of investigation.

In spite of striking similarities with the findings of other studies on NGO intervention (Guéneau, 1984; Crombrugge et al., 1985; Lecompte, 1986), extrapolation of the findings of this study alone to the whole NGO universum is certainly not warranted. Concerning the Indonesian study, it was not possible to confirm the representativity of findings for the whole area of intervention of Bina Swadaya, while the Thai study focussing on success villages had no such pretention. The limitations of the study's outcome as to representativity and generalizability for NGO interventions in general are caused by:

– the limited number of SHPIs/NGOs participating in the study, i.e. three research sites;

– the absence of any effort to establish the representativity of SHPIs within the sample; SHPIs were selected on the basis of their relationship with one particular donor NGO (Cebemo) and the level of economic activities they are involved in through the SHOs which they promote.

Further limitations result from the following considerations:

– Conclusions about the mutual relationship and causation between system elements are based mainly on the subjective perceptions of research participants: households, group members, local leaders, researchers, SHPI staff. Some quantitative data have supported the interpretative process but the more general conclusions which have been arrived at do not lend themselves to objective verification. To the extent that there is consensus among the various actors in the research process, the validity of the findings can be said to be based on 'intersubjectivity'. Further, the whole research process, in spite of its participative nature, was managed by the local NGO research teams who were also responsible for drafting the country research reports. Their personal interpretation of reality as a team will unavoidably strongly affect the presentation of the findings. The same applies to the contribution by the Cebemo research coordinator in synthesizing the findings. It should be realized that in this type of research dealing with such a value-loaded concept as self-help, it is extremely difficult to remain free from personal prejudice.

– The 'self' of self-evaluation in the context of this study relates to the organization and not to the persons involved in the process. Even so, the study put high demands on the integrity and capacity for objectivity of research participants who have an ongoing working relationship with the SHPI/local NGO whose methods of work are being assessed. However, the critical overtones of the Brazilian and Indonesian studies in particular seem to testify to such capacity. Above all, there is the issue of 'confidentiality' of certain information which we shall discuss in the next chapter.

4   Problems encountered in the study's implementation

By associating the practitioners of self-help promotion, i.e. local leaders, ordinary SHO members, and SHPI staff with the research process, it was attempted to circumvent the classical dichotomy between researchers and practitioners, and heighten the relevance of the findings and the likelihood of follow-up action. The value of this approach was recognized by the participant SHPIs. However, it also generated a series of methodological and practical problems. To take a close and critical look at such problems is important in view of the growing interest in externally assisted self-evaluation as a tool of organizational change, and the possible replication of the present study in other settings.

Maturation of the idea
The study, as stated earlier, was initiated by a Dutch based non-governmental financing agency, Cebemo, which had been giving support to the participant SHPIs over a number of years. In none of the cases in the three countries is Cebemo the SHPI's major source of finance. In the Indonesian and Brazilian cases, it only supplements more substantial contributions from other agencies. Even so, a proposal from a 'donor' agency inviting a local NGO to engage itself in an extensive review of its own strategy and working methods is bound, in the first instance, to cause some uneasiness with at least part of the staff of the local NGO. Such feelings may even be shared by some of the staff of the donor agency, especially those who in the past have been closely associated with the appraisal and approval of projects requested by the SHPI concerned. A whole hearted endorsement of the idea on the part of the local SHPI will understandably only be forthcoming after it has assured itself that, irrespective of the study's outcome, it can count on continuing moral and financial support from the overseas agency, within the limits, of course, of what the study would yield in terms of desirable and recommendable follow-up activities. The study's idea has to mature, and the design and orientation of the study will need adjustment to suit local conditions and priorities. All this takes time.

Conceptual confusion
Another set of problems relates to the concepts used for the present study. Concepts like self-help, self-reliance, promotion, target population, etc., belong to the international vernacular of development professionals and cannot easily be translated into languages embedded in a different culture (Brazilian-Portuguese, Bahasa Indonesia, Thai). Such concepts may provoke animated discussions between experts at the international level, but may be void of meaning in the local setting if not transposed, rather than translated, into concepts and terms

that make sense in the local languages. In fact, the leaders of the local action-research teams had a hard job in 'translating' the working documents prepared by the Cebemo research coordinator and making them understandable for discussion with the other members of the team less familiar with academic English. In particular, a concept like 'self-help' proved problematic and could only be explained in a descriptive manner because of lack of a good equivalent in any of the other languages. For a 'participatory' study it is legitimate to raise the question whether such a study can claim to be that if it is not explicitly based on concepts and terms which originate from the milieu of the SHO members and leadership. The problem of inter-cultural communication can never be solved in an entirely satisfactory manner for all parties concerned. However, a greater awareness of the cultural dimension when defining concepts would certainly have raised the level of 'self-help' of the research exercise itself.

Less problematic proved to be the idea of a systems approach and the corresponding framework as a means to integrate findings which emerged from the study at different levels and at different times. Its acceptance implies recognition of the circular and complex causality of relationships and events – 'everything is related to everything' – which is much nearer to reality and to the life experience of practitioners than the linear patterns of reasoning used in the conventional type of study.

Confidentiality of information
Since the study was action-based and participatory, this meant that some research team members, in their capacity of SHPI employees, were asked to study the effectiveness of their own work and organization. Under such conditions, their intimate knowledge of the situation could only bear fruit if they were capable of self-criticism, and if such an attitude was positively valued by both peers and superiors. Such an ideal situation rarely exists in an absolute manner. Each organization has its own set of problems which staff consider it improper or unacceptable to discuss openly – let alone report to outsiders – but which still have an impact on strategy and methods of work. It should therefore be borne in mind that country reports and, in consequence, the integrated report may have omitted to mention some important internal constraints of the various SHPIs or SHOs. This does not imply that they have not been considered at all, since it is the experience of the participant NGOs that the very undertaking of the study has facilitated the discussion of some sensitive issues which would have remained undiscussed otherwise. The possible lack of objectivity and the existence of such organizational taboos and secrets do not outweigh the advantages of incorporation of practitioners in the research teams. For studies of this nature, we should bear in mind that the purpose is not to disclose the unveiled naked truth and expose it mercilessly to the outside world, but to provide local NGOs with an opportunity to raise their level of competence and effectiveness.

Outside support is necessary for the analysis of internal weaknesses
A further problem generated by the nature of the study, arose from the close correlation that exists between promotional and analytical capabilities. A SHPI cannot be expected to have analytical skill in a field where its promotional practice has suffered from a lack of expertise. For example, a SHPI which in the past has been unable to provide sufficient assistance to enable SHOs to carry out economic feasibility studies for proposed micro-projects, will also lack the

capacity for assessing the viability of ongoing activities and their impact on member economies. Outside support in such cases is necessary to compensate for the SHPI's limitations. This has become very apparent in the Brazilian case. In spite of such outside support, the financial analysis of SHO activities could not be conducted at the desired depth because of the weak data basis. The prevailing accounting system precluded making a clear distinction between variable and fixed costs, and the allocation of the general items of expenditure to the various economic activities was complicated by lack of sufficient precision about the relationship between the two. Such limitations notwithstanding, the results were revealing, not least for the SHPI concerned.

In self-evaluation there is thus a tendency for SHPIs to focus attention on those aspects of their work in which they feel strongest, while the weaker, less developed aspects which perhaps merit focal attention, may remain under-researched or not studied at all.

This can be further illustrated by the way in which phases 2 and 3 of the study were conducted in the Thai case. The Thai study carefully analysed processes of self-help organization and action in two success villages (phase 3). It yielded highly interesting case material in relation to those aspects of their work which are the most developed, but another aspect of their work – more sensitive, somewhat neglected, yet of special importance in the Thai situation –, namely inter-NGO collaboration (phase 2), was not analysed.

Different objectives

The initiating agency, Cebemo, wished to use the study to get a better insight into institutional collaboration, viz. between the SHPIs and other supporting institutions. Such collaboration was assumed to be important if self-help promotion were to become a major tool for socio-economic change that would surpass the boundaries of the micro- (village) level, and also have an effect on meso- and macro-level structures. For a well thought-out SH promotion strategy, it is necessary to know what other agencies are doing, or are planning to do, and drawing them into the research process was one of the objectives of study. This worked out differently in practice. The systematic collection of information on the operations of supporting organizations proved cumbersome and time-consuming and did not provide the SHPI with any new insights. For the participant SHPIs, improving the effectiveness of their own organization (or Catholic sister organizations, Thailand) was their main concern. The other elements of the study, viz. analysis of SHO performance, general village and specific household surveys, and the systematic analysis of the applied self-help promotion instrumentarium, were found useful and helpful, but not the collection of detailed information on what other organizations in the same area, sometimes with the same objectives, were doing. A similar orientation became apparent in the follow-up programmes which assert the SHPI's intention to improve upon their own working methods as a matter of priority, but do not specifically mention the search for better coordination between local agencies at regional level.

A NGO cannot investigate a governmental organization

The undertaking of phase 2 of the study was further complicated by the often strained relations between government and non-governmental agencies. Data collection on the operations of government agencies is not possible without official clearance from the agencies' headquarters, mostly based in the capital, which takes too long, is too complicated and may stir up questions which may endanger the whole study undertaking. This was therefore dispensed with. In the case of Indonesia and Brazil, information on government agency operations could be obtained informallly, which is the way in which government and non-governmental agents normally communicate at field level. In the Thai study, the relationship between the DISACs and other supporting agencies was analysed only indirectly, to the extent that activites of other agencies had a direct bearing on those of the SHOs in the two research villages.

Instruments not used cannot be analysed
A problem of a different nature occurred in the Indonesian case, one month after the commencement of phase 3 of the study which included the analysis of the operations of SHOs at village level. In the course of the research it became increasingly clear that the rural poor living in the selected village cluster of Baleharjo were only marginally involved in the activities of the SHOs promoted by BS. In order to be able to gain better insight into the relationship between SHO activities and the economy of the rural poor, the action-researchers considered, rightly, that the study should be extended to a second cluster of villages where the involvement of the rural poor in organized self-help was expected to be greater. The low level of involvement of the poor majority in the first village cluster was in itself an important finding, since this had not previously been realized by the field staff. It illustrated an important shortcoming in the SHPI's instrumentation, viz. the absence of 'identification of the target population' as a systematically organized practice, well integrated into work habits and orientation of the average Bina Swadaya field worker. However, the study of the effectiveness of the *use* of this instrument, as envisaged by the study, was now impracticable. Where there is no action, one cannot study its effects, only the possible consequences of its absence. But the need for the instrument's introduction became abundantly clear, and the study itself provided some indication of how this could be undertaken. Similar situations occurred in the other two countries where instruments were found to be missing, not well integrated or under-utilized, and where such findings prompted a discussion on the appropriateness of their introduction or improvement.

Scope of the study too broad for the time available
The origin of another category of problems can be traced back to the study's time budget. The present study was organized as an interdisciplinary, multi-level, multi-focus study: multi-level because it was undertaken at SHPI, SHO (village), and household level and, in a later stage, its findings had to be interpreted on their implications for local NGO – donor NGO relationship; multi-focus because it studied a wide range of topics and centred on the study of not less than eight self-help promotion instruments as part of an integrated self-help promotion system.

53

It was the general feeling of the action-researchers that the time allocated for the study in the three countries, i.e. six months, was too short. Even the time eventually taken, on average nine months, was too short if one takes into account that practically all members of the three research teams had other duties to attend to during the study, and could only make themselves available on a part-time basis. More time, for example, would have been required to take full advantage of the opportunity, provided by the household surveys, for direct contact with the rural poor. These household surveys, conducted in an informal dialogue atmosphere were, in fact, the only means for the poor to participate more directly in the research process, given the well-known domination of leadership during group discussions. The poor carry with them a wealth of experience and information, but they may be reluctant to release it or have difficulty in conveying it in a manner which can be understood by the action-researchers. Better integration in the research process could have been achieved not so much by covering more households, but by spreading visits over a longer period of time (three to four months instead of one), and increasing the number of visits (eight to ten instead of three to four).

The same applies to the extension of the study to other localities which, because of the time constraint, had to be done somewhat hurriedly through workshops with leaders, and with insufficient opportunity for cross-checking with other sources of information such as informal talks, group interviews and direct observations in villages other than the selected ones.

On the question of time, it would have been better if participant NGOs had been given the opportunity to select from the general study's framework a few topics for priority investigation, and to move on from there as part of an ongoing research exercise. But from the viewpoint of the overseas agency (Cebemo), which initiated the study simultaneously in three countries, this would have been less attractive as it would have weakened the comparative basis of the study and prolonged its undertaking for an indeterminate period. On the other hand, from the SHPIs' perspective, such an arrangement would have been more satisfactory. In practice, some sort of compromise was found in each of the countries.

The Thai study, as stated, concentrated on the process of self-help organization as materialized at village level, and the catalytic role of the SHPI in that process. The cultural dimension of self-help promotion was given more prominent attention than in other studies.

The Brazilian study, during the second half of the research period, focussed strongly on economic feasibility and prospects for SHOs to generate sufficient revenues to cover long-term costs.

The Indonesian study, by following the research design meticulously, was fairly comprehensive, except that due to shortage of time and expertise in specific fields, action-researchers were unable to cover all topics in equal depth. For the same reasons, participation of the target population in the analysis could not be as intensive as researchers had wished (Indonesian report, p. 129).

The principal merit of the present study appears to be that it has made an important contribution to improved effectiveness of self-help promotion in the three countries where this was studied. For this process to keep its momentum, analysis and reflection will have to become part of an ongoing exercise. We have discussed this earlier as instrument no. 8: i.e. 'monitoring and ongoing evaluation' (Chapter 3). Ensuring that this will happen is the main function of the intended follow-up programmes.

Major lessons learnt
The major lessons learnt from the problems as discussed above can be summarized as follows:
– When a foreign agency seeks to elicit the interest of its overseas partners in undertaking a participatory self-evaluative study, it might be appropriate to

initiate the idea on the basis of a conceptual framework phrased in an international language. In the present case this was English. However, prior to drafting the study's plan of operation and starting field research, it is necessary to rethink and adjust both the concepts and the conceptual framework in a direction which will ensure that the basic notions underlying the study's 'problematic' can be easily understood by the average non-English speaking fieldworker. We could call this process the 'cultural adjustment' of the concepts and conceptual framework.

– A comprehensive framework is recommended to facilitate the identification of study topics. But within this broad framework clear priorities will have to be set, taking into consideration time, manpower and financial constraints. The research programme should evolve gradually at each stage, taking into consideration the findings and experiences of the earlier stage. Setting of priorities was also done under the present study, but more through force of circumstances than as an organized practice.

– The phasing of research activities as illustrated in figure 7 in the previous chapter is neither wrong nor necessarily the best. One could for example very well conceive a study which starts at household level and from there moves upwards to study the functioning of SHOs, SHPI(s) and their interface (instruments). One could as well, depending on circumstances and priorities, focus first on the economic aspects, branching out later into the political, social and/or cultural dimensions, or vice versa.

– Local NGOs normally will need outside assistance on a regular basis from academically trained local researchers, to steer and coordinate the self-evaluation process. In those fields where SHPI and SHO performance seem weakest, the need for outside assistance will be greatest, although at the outset this might not always be easily recognized by the SHPI concerned.

Location of research area, Gunung Kidul District, in the Special Territory (Province) of Yogyakarta, Java.

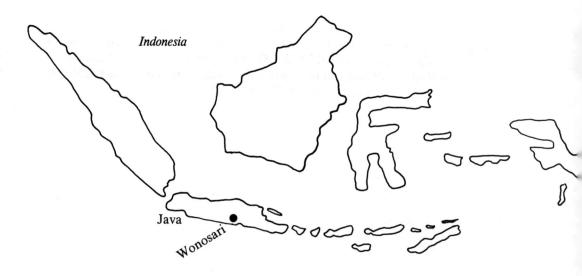

Indonesia

Java

Wonosari

Part II

Study findings and conclusions

Location of research areas, Sisaket Province in the northeast and Chomthong District near the city of Chiengmai in north Thailand.

Location of research area, Serrinha 'Municipio' (District) in the State of Bahia, northeast Brazil.

5 Research areas and villages; a description

The following is a short description of the areas and villages where the study took place. It has been limited to highlighting just a few of the most outstanding features which were found to influence the SHPI and SHO activities and performance analysed later in this chapter.

In Brazil, the study took place primarily in Serrinha district (Municipio), situated some 180 kilometers to the east from the coastal city of Salvador, the capital of the state of Bahia in the northeast of the country.

The Indonesian research area, Gunung Kidul district, is one of the five districts of the Special Province of Yogyakarta in Middle Java.

In Thailand, the study was undertaken in two different parts of the country: in the northeast in Sisaket Province where the study focussed on the village of Ban Isan*; and in the north, not far from its main city Chiengmai, in Chomthong district, with a focus on the village of Ban Nua*.

Some common features and differences

The research areas selected in the three countries are all situated in regions with a well developed infrastructure and good connections to major cities. Another common characteristic is their poor resource endowment for agricultural production, caused by low soil fertility and chronic water shortage, alternating with irregular, torrential rains often causing floods. The only exception is one of the two selected sites in Thailand, Chomthong district, in the northern region, where rainfall is more regular and rice is cultivated on terraces. However, land holdings here are very small (on average 0.5 hectare) and nearly half the population is landless.

Another feature shared by research areas in the selected countries is the large number of smallholders whose holdings tend to become even smaller in every generation. They are the main 'target group' of the three SHPIs. At the same time the number of landless families is growing, most of whom have no other choice than to look for seasonal employment outside the village as unskilled and low-paid labourers, or to migrate permanently to the city slums. Such trends are well known and characteristic of 'rural development' in many developing countries,

*Names of villages are fictitious.

and the research areas and villages in the three countries covered by this study are no exception to this rule. A major difference between the research areas is the pattern of land distribution. In Brazil, the division of landownership is much more skewed than in the two Asian countries. Landlessness was found to exist in all cases, but more prominently in the Brazil research area (35%) and in the north of Thailand (45%) than in Thailand's northeast and in the Indonesian research areas.

Brazil

Serrinha district is situated in Bahia State, at the heart of the northeast region. The northeast is reputedly the poorest part of the country, characterized by excessive inequality of land distribution (5% of the landholders hold 95% of the land) and a high rate of illiteracy (75%). Serrinha district counts 50,000 inhabitants, half of whom live in Serrinha town, the district's capital, the other half being spread over 17 'comunidades' in rural areas. Subaé, the selected research village, is one of these. Between 1970 – 1980 the pattern of land distribution has become even more unequal. The average landholding in Serrinha district, within the category 0 to 10 hectares, went down from 4.4 hectares to 2.8 hectares, while the number of landholdings belonging to this lowest category rose from 71% to 79% (Brazilian report, p. 79). During the same period the number of landholdings of over 200 hectares increased by 25%, as did the total area occupied by the so-called 'fazendeiros'. The 'fazendeiros' use their land principally for cattle breeding and fattening. 35% of the rural families are landless. They depend entirely on wage labour. The minimum salary amounts to Cruzados 25 (approx. US$ 2) per day, but most workers, particularly if they are female, receive less. The main crops cultivated in Serrinha area are cassava, maize, beans (feijâo) and sisal. With a rainfall averaging 900 to 1,000 mm per year Serrinha is better off than most other places in the northeast. The most powerful person in the district is the 'Prefeito'. He is known for his conservative outlook and supports the cause of the 'fazendeiros'. In Serrinha district, the latter also control the administration of the Rural Trade Union. Though not supportive of MOC's promotional work, the 'Prefeito' is constitutionally bound to tolerate the operations of MOC and of the farmer organization APAEB, which is the main target organization of MOC's intervention. The research village, the 'comunidade' of Subaé, comprises 81 households of which more than two-thirds (59) are sympathetic to, and members of, APAEB, while the remainder identify themselves rather with the conservative faction led by the village mayor and a conservative priest.
There is however no sharp split between the two groups nor are there major differences in socio-economic status. The average landholding centres around 6.5 hectares (15 tarefas). Over one-third of the village households are landless.

60

Indonesia

The Indonesian research area, Gunung Kidul district in Middle Java, has its administrative and commercial centre in a small town, Wonosari, situated at some 40 kms to the east of Yogyakarta city. Ninety-five per cent of the district's population live in rural areas.

Taking into account the poor quality of its soil and water resources, the population density of the district at 466 per square km is still very high but not extraordinary by Javanese standards. About 42% of the population are illiterate. Its main agricultural products are cassava, padigogo (dry-field rice), sweet potatoes, peanuts, soja beans and peas. The main food crop is cassava; only the well-to-do families can afford to eat rice every day. Cattle breeding and raising is widespread under the 'Penggaduhan' system. (The owner buys the cattle, the 'Penggaduhan' has to take care of all aspects such as stable, food, medicine, etc. After the cattle are sold the gross profit will be divided at the rate of 50%–50%. Calves are shared on the same basis.)

The study took place at two sites within the district, not far from the district capital Wonosari. One was in the 'Kelurahan' of Baleharjo, a cluster of five villages comprising 936 households. When it was found that most of the Usaha Bersama (UB) membership in this village could not be numbered among the rural poor, a second site was selected, Pacing, which is somewhat further from Wonosari (8 km), and comprises 214 households. Most of the villagers in Pacing are 'abangas', officially registered Moslems who in fact practise the Javanese traditional religion. In Baleharjo Christianity is more widespread (50%), particularly among the better-off.

One of the most remarkable features of Baleharjo – and this is typical of the Indonesian setting – is the huge number of informal and formal groups which shape day-to-day interaction between villagers in the socio-economic and cultural spheres of life. The action researchers counted over 250 groups for 930 households (sports, cultural and religious groups not included). Of the 250 groups 56 are 'arisan' (the traditional savings and credit association), and 73 'dasa wisma' (neighbourhood groups of 10 houses). Most groups, including 6 Usaha Bersama (UBs), pre-cooperatives supported by Bina Swadaya, operate in the socio-economic field while others are active in the field of agriculture, education, health and nutrition. (Indonesian report, pp. A-6 and A-7).

There is a direct relation between a person's status and the number of groups to which he belongs. The higher a person's rank, the larger the number of groups to which he (she) contributes. The village cluster Baleharjo is also studded with small shops (about 100), not counting the numerous small street vendors. In the other research village, Pacing, no systematic recording of existing groups was done but there are far fewer government-initiated groups. There are only two small shops and no street vendors.

Thailand

As discussed in chapter 4, the Thai study had an even more pronounced village focus than the other two countries.

Ban Isan village is situated in one of the poorest areas of northeast Thailand. But it is still affluent when compared with other villages in the same province of Sisaket. The average landholding in Ban Isan amounts to 30 Rai (4.8 hectares), which is nearly twice as much as the average for the northeast. Landlessness in this part of the country is still exceptional. Most Ban Isan villagers are literate, an exceptional situation for northeast Thailand. The relatively easy access to school facilities can be explained by the villagers' affiliation to the Catholic church. The conversion to Catholicism took place about 70 years ago when the village was founded. Ban Isan's founding fathers opted for Catholicism to escape their

'Phibob' status. Phibob are outcasts believed to be beset by some sort of evil spirit and for that reason are pressed to leave the village. This explains that even today nearly the whole village population is Catholic, which puts it in a rather special situation since Catholicism is practised in Thailand by a tiny minority (only 0.5%).

The village numbers 200 households, 70 of which are involved in DISAC-supported self-help group activities. Rice is the main crop, while additional cash income is obtained from growing cassava (which in Thailand is not a food crop), jute and vegetables. Like every Thai village Ban Isan has its committees: a Village Development committee, a Church committee (the equivalent of the Temple committee in a Buddhist village), an Education committee (a sort of parents' advisory board for the primary school), a Funeral committee, Drama and/or Music group, etc. Ban Isan was elected as a village for study because it is engaged in a range of successfully conducted self-help activities. But the methodology of self-help promotion which DISAC Ubon has developed on the basis of its experiences in Ban Isan and other villages, is now generally applied to all 'DISAC villages', irrespective of the religious status of their residents.

The other Thai village, Ban Nua, is located in north Thailand. Its population is Buddhist. The main crop is irrigated rice, part of which is grown under a share-cropping system (yield and costs are divided on a fifty-fifty per cent basis between owner and sharecropper). Landholdings vary between two and eight Rai (less than 0.3 hectares to 1.3 hectares). 27 out of the 120 households are landless, which is rather low by north Thailand standards (45%). They live by occasional wage labour and on what they can get out of the forest, such as firewood, mushrooms, indigenous vegetables, etc., which they exchange for rice or sell on the local market. Ban Nua is a village rather typical for north Thailand. The increasing land scarcity is creating a worrisome situation for the villagers. In spite of frequent seasonal migration, social cohesion is still strong. Village life is at its height during religious ceremonies, which play a crucial role in preventing social disintegration.

Brazil – peeling of cassava roots by women prior to milling. The mill belongs to the Association of Small Farmers.

Thailand – small farmer households earn some additional income from off-farm occupations, like silkworm rearing, spinning and weaving, but middlemen cut into the profit.

63

Indonesia – a tenant livestock-farmer. A loan from the UB group will enable him to become the owner of the animal he is fattening.

6   Self-help promotion institutions in the three countries compared

In this chapter we shall review and compare the history, structure, functions, linkages and development dilemmas of the four SHPIs (MOC, Bina Swadaya and the two DISACs) which have participated in the action-research.

The analysis will be carried out from the double perspective of 'organizational survival' and self-help promotion. The first, organizational survival, is one of the informal objectives of any organization, SHPI not excluded. It refers to the concern of SHPI staff to make their organization survive and perpetuate its functions in a competitive environment: competition which may come from other NGOs in the pursuance of their own organizational objectives and strategies, or from other institutions, governmental or private, which are inimical to, or suspicious of, NGO intervention.

The second perspective, self-help promotion, is a development objective. It implies, as someone at the Thailand workshop put it, that 'the DISAC (the SHPI) should become less and that the self-help organizations, the organizations of the people, should grow'. These two objectives, one organizational, the other developmental, are difficult to reconcile and may easily get SHPIs into a dilemma from which there is no easy way out.

History of the SHPIs in the three countries

MOC, the Movimento de Organização Comunitaria, in Brazil started nineteen years ago as the welfare branch of the diocese of Feira de Santana. In the course of years it has changed its statute, objectives and methods of work. In 1970 it became an autonomous secular legal entity. Its development orientation changed gradually from 'assistencialismo' towards self-help promotion both in the economic and political fields.

The Indonesian *Bina Swadaya* organization became a legal entity only in March 1985, but its roots are nearly thirty years old. In 1958 the Pancasila Farmers' Movement (Itatan Petani Pancasila, IPP) was founded to assist farmers with agricultural training and legal matters. IPP also started the promotion of UB groups. In 1967, IPP established the Peasants Socio-Economic Development Foundation (Yayasan Sosial Tani Membangun, YSTM) to carry out projects which were directed towards the economically weak rural communities. Over the past ten years the YSTM has grown rapidly and developed several 'Centres of

Activity' in the fields of training, agricultural production, processing, and printing. One of these Centres, named PUSBINUB, focusses on the promotion of pre-cooperatives, called UBs (Usaha Bersama = 'joint efforts'). It is this Centre which participated in the present study. YSTM still continues to function as a publishing agency but the activities of all the other Centres were brought together under a new foundation, 'Bina Swadaya' (Agency for Community Self-Reliance Development). In fact the above description of organizational development of Bina Swadaya is very much simplified. Its history has constituted a very careful balancing act in the grey area between what is and what is not permitted by an autocratic government, a process in which diplomatic skills carry more weight than legal status or rights.

The founding fathers of the Pancasila Farmers' Movement in the fifties had close ties with the Catholic Church, but YSTM and its offshoot Bina Swadaya have pursued a policy of neutrality with regard to religious denominations.

The 'Law on Mass Organizations', which received parliamentary approval in May 1986, has made the adoption of Pancasila*, the consensus-building state ideology, obligatory for all development organizations, including Bina Swadaya. Non-compliance, in theory or in practice, will inevitably provoke an organization's disbandment.

Unlike MOC and Bina Swadaya, which have secular status, the Catholic Council of Thailand for Development (CCTD) is formally attached to the Catholic Church. The CCTD was formed in 1970 as one of the commissions of the Office for Social Affairs of the Bishops' conference. It acts as an umbrella organization for Catholic Organizations operating in the field of social welfare and development. The impetus for Church-related organizations to become more development-oriented had come in the early sixties from Vatican II (1962 – 1965). At the time the main focus in the economic field was on the creation of 'credit unions', a special type of savings and credit cooperative.

Credit unions have since formed their own national organization: the Credit Union League of Thailand. In the seventies the CCTD Secretariat encouraged the Dioceses to set up their own development units. Ten so-called *DISACs* (Diocese Social Action Centres) were established and two of them, namely the DISAC of Ubon and DISAC Chiengmai, participated in the present study.

The Thai research report records how the policy and perspective of these two DISACs have changed over the years from a paternalistic to a more participatory style of intervention, and from a narrow economistic to a more holistic approach. Most groups started as 'recipient' groups of DISAC assistance. Aid was given to meet the urgency of the situation caused by some sort of calamity such as a bad harvest. Parish priests wrote project proposals without much preliminary consultation with the intended beneficiaries. Monetary assistance was given without obligation of repayment. It was centred on Catholic minority groups. But in the eighties the methods of work have undergone a dramatic change, later to be discussed in detail.

65

---

* The five pillars of Pancasila are in short: belief in one God; humanity; Indonesian unity; democracy; social justice. In practice wide interpretation of these principles is allowed as long as development practice does not go against official government policy.

Objectives of the SHPIs

All four participating SHPIs in the three countries are committed to long-range development and the promotion of Self-Help Organizations, especially among the economically weaker sections of the population. A comparison of the formal objectives of the SHPIs does not reveal significant differences in orientation. Much more interesting is the comparison of informal, long term objectives which are far more relevant in explaining the course of action taken by the respective SHPIs.

MOC's development aim is predominantly political, aimed at changing the present power structure through a variety of interventions, not directly related to party politics. Such a stand would be inconceivable in the Indonesian context and perilous in the Thai situation if shown too openly. MOC wishes to contribute to the construction of a more 'egalitarian' society. The present societal structure is regarded as unjust and in need of dramatic change. MOC therefore supports the progressive forces within the rural trade unions ('Sindicatos'). Over the past years MOC has been giving increased attention to the promotion of economic activities by self-help groups. The activities undertaken in the political and economic field are viewed as mutually reinforcing.

MOC has never envisaged the undertaking of commercial activities for the purpose of generating its own income. It does not pursue the financial autonomy of its own organization but tries to further the economic self-reliance of the target population, including the latter's organizations such as APAEB (the association of small producers of the state of Bahia) and other affiliated groups. In this respect, its policy is noticeably different from the Indonesian *Bina Swadaya* which has been encouraged by one of its main German donor organizations to boost its own income-generating capacities to such an extent that the organization can stand on its own feet, financially. With the exception of the field department PUSBINUB, all the other Bina Swadaya departments ('Centres') are now indeed more or less self-financing.

The development aim of the two *DISACs* in Thailand is to promote a value-system, not economic development per se. Economic activities are regarded as possibly helpful in this process but they can also be counter-productive, depending on the sort of values which underlie the functioning of the organization and keep it going. If an economic activity is potentially profitable but in the cultural sphere has no other effect than to promote greed, individualism, and consumerism among the participants, it does not merit support by the DISAC. As we shall see in chapter 9, this approach has important consequences for the type of economic activities which receive DISAC support as well as for the rules and regulations which govern their functioning.

Target population and target areas

The target population of the rural programme of *MOC* consists of small farmers and their families. They are holders of small, sometimes very small plots of land of insufficient size or quality to feed the family and generate the necessary additional monetary income. MOC's focus is on the poorest 85% of the rural population (the upper limit is up to 20 hectares of dry farm land). Members of the SHOs promoted by MOC belong to the poor majority, but at the same time MOC, as it says in its report, has not yet been able to develop an effective mechanism to reach out to the 'poorest of the poor', most of whom are landless. MOC's area of operations was identical with that of the Diocese of Feira de Santana, viz. thirty 'Municipios' (districts). Actually MOC has limited its action-radius to fourteen of them and to approximately 100 'comunidades' (village groups). This means that, within each of the fourteen districts, MOC covers only a small part of the existing villages. In the district of Serrinha, one of MOC's concentration areas, MOC is active in 17 villages. The Serrinha groups have altogether 400 members, which means that MOC through its promotional work is directly or indirectly in touch with about 10% of the rural families living in the Serrinha district. In the other districts the coverage is much less. MOC also has an urban programme which is less significant and is not discussed in this study. Although officially the target population of *Bina Swadaya* consists of the rural poor, in practice UB membership is drawn from the entire rural population, including village teachers, small entrepreneurs, male and female skilled and unskilled workers, small fishermen, etc. The approximately 450 UB groups are scattered all over Java and south Sumatra. Seven of them are situated in Gunung Kidul district where the study took place, involving 658 households, which is less than 0.5% of the rural families of that district area.

The huge areas of operation of the *DISACs* of Chiengmai and Ubon in Thailand each comprise six provinces ('Changwat'). The average province covers between 0.5 million and 1.5 million persons. The DISAC of Chiengmai supports 120 projects running in 89 villages, and the DISAC of Ubon 147 in 40 villages, involving on average 30 households per village. The villages are at large distances from each other. The coverage in Thai cases can also be estimated at less than 0.5% of the rural population.

The target population of the DISAC of Chiengmai in north Thailand comprises two main categories: the economically backward hill tribes which are poorly integrated into Thai society and the poor rural Thai communities. The present study has concentrated on the second category to allow comparison with the methods of work of the other Thai SHPI, the DISAC Ubon. Both DISACs are deliberately moving away from exclusive attention to Christian villages or groups. In doing so, however, they are somewhat handicapped by suspicion on the part of Buddhist fundamentalists – a minority within the Buddhist upper clergy – who tend to view this liberal attitude as a change of strategy in Christian missionary practice.

The reason for giving the approximate figures on 'coverage' mentioned above is not to minimize the importance of the work being done by the participant SHPIs, but to illustrate the difficulties local NGOs have in raising the standards of living of the rural poor on a significant geographical scale and making impact on processes of socio-economic change at the meso/regional level.

Organizational structure

Of the participant SHPIs, *MOC* has the simplest structure. It is a single unit of 23 persons of whom 11 are academically trained. It has its headquarters at Feira de

Santana and a small branch at 70 km distance at Serrinha, the selected research area. The division of responsibilities among staff members has been made in a way which avoids the usual dichotomy between field and administrative staff. The MOC principle of non-specialization of office and field work is also practised, implicitly, by the two DISACs in Thailand. By law MOC is an association. In practice the real decision-making powers reside with the executive secretary and his team.

The much larger Indonesian *Bina Swadaya*, employing nearly 200 persons, has a much more complex structure. It operates as a federation of semi-autonomous 'Centres', which in the course of the years have all developed their own range of income generating activities: the 'education and training centre' (Pusdiklat) through the fees it charges for attendance at its courses; the Centre for Production and Marketing services (Pusprosar) by its involvement in various projects and enterprises, including a slaughterhouse and a shrimp hatchery; the Centre for Research and Development (Puslitbang) through its studies for third parties on a consultancy basis; and, finally, the Publication Centre (Pusbitan) through the publication of the most prestigious Indonesian agriculture magazine 'Trubus' (directed at a middle-class readership) and a series of booklets on agricultural techniques. A newly created Centre, the Centre for Solidarity Capital Formation (Pusdaya) will manage, at national level, the savings and credit programmes for the affiliated UB groups. This Centre is also intended to become self-financing. The present study is only concerned with the activities of the Centre for Pre-cooperative Development, PUSBINUB. This has a staff of six people stationed at Jakarta headquarters and 18 field workers spread over Java and south Sumatra, most of them working under direct supervision from the central office. The Yogyakarta branch, which carried out the present study, counts four workers in addition to one foreign 'integrated expert' and one coordinator. PUSBINUB has participated much less in the extension of the BS organization of the past ten years, nor does the nature of its work lend itself very much to income generation.

The *CCTD* of Thailand is a federation of 35 Catholic organizations. Among them are ten Diocesan Social Action Centres (DISACs) which have been set up in the ten Thai dioceses parallel to the structure of the Catholic church. Their autonomy is quite well illustrated by the fact that the decision whether or not to participate in the present study was taken by the directors of the two participating DISACs, following consultations with their staff. The DISAC staffs are small: one director-priest and three lay field workers of high-school educational background. Every field worker covers 15 to 30 villages, a number comparable to the number of UB groups assisted by the Bina Swadaya workers. However, the position of the Thai field workers in the SHPI's organizational hierarchy is different. The Thai field workers, especially those attached to the diocese of Chiengmai, have a greater say in the determination of organizational policies than their Indonesian counterparts. This does not alter the fact that the procedures for policy determination within PUSBINUB, through yearly evaluation sessions, are still very democratic compared to other Indonesian NGOs.

The MOC action-researchers also regard the sort of field workers' self-management system as practised by the DISAC Chiengmai as ideal, but it cannot always be realized since 'bossy' behaviour seems deeply rooted in Brazilian culture. Top-down rule within an organization is normally mirrored by top-down methods of work in the field. It is this consideration which makes the participation of field workers in policy determination such an important organizational feature of SHPIs.

Development functions

Development functions can be distinguished according to: sector of activity; roles played by the SHPI; specific instruments as applied by the SHPI in carrying out its development tasks.
The instruments will be considered in greater detail in Chapter 8. Here we shall review sectors and roles.

MOC – Brazil
MOC's promotional work in rural areas has four main dimensions:
– The promotion of ecologically sound agricultural techniques;
– The promotion of economic activities through APAEB and affiliated groups;
– Support of the progressive forces within the rural trade unions ('Sindicatos');
– Health care and promotion of the use of natural medicine.
The activities are conceived as mutually supportive. APAEB is conceived as the economic leg of a political movement. MOC's role in supporting the trade union movement is to organize training sessions for its leadership and to be available for advice if and when the need arises. After some earlier experiments MOC's involvement in economic activities ('projects') has become more determined since 1978.
In its annual report (1985) MOC stresses that it has no economic projects of its own but wants to support the projects of APAEB and other groups. APAEB's economic activities will be analysed in Chapter 7. APAEB's main activities are the processing and storage of basic food crops and the operation of consumer shops.

Bina Swadaya – Indonesia
Bina Swadaya, as we have seen, through its various 'Centres' has branched out into a great variety of activities. In this report we shall consider only the work of the field department PUSBINUB which concentrates on two closely related development functions:
– To provide self-help groups in rural areas, called UBs*, with some simple tools to administer their savings and credit operations.
– To provide UBs with additional capital from a centrally managed so-called 'Solidarity Fund'. This credit programme (KSK) started in 1976. Credits disbursed since then amount to a total of Rps 478 million (US$ 425,000). In the period January to December 1985 credits amounting to Rps 87 million US$ 77,000) were disbursed to 58 UB groups. The rate of repayment is high: 98%! Substantial donor support allows the amount of disbursements to increase every year.
As we shall see below, groups which have adopted the UB administrative system vary a lot in terms of objectives, composition of membership, and internal organization. Over the past two years, some of these groups have been encouraged by BS to branch out and undertake economic activities in the fields of agricultural production, processing, handicrafts or trade. They are supposed to

---

* UB = Usaha Bersama or 'Joint Efforts'

undertake such activities as a group. However, a recently started project in the Yogyakarta area has opted for a different strategy. This KAS*-supported project envisages providing investment credit to individual entrepreneurs using UBs as a channel for the transfer of monies.

The DISACs – Thailand
The DISAC of Chiengmai in northern Thailand shares with MOC, Brazil, its great interest in the promotion of alternative, organic types of agriculture. The reasons for pursuing such a course are threefold:
– ecological concern;
– economical advantage because of lower costs of agricultural inputs;
– less or no dependence of farmers on external suppliers of chemical fertilizers and pesticides as well as on credit from financing organizations.
The underlying philosophy is that it is not man's vocation to conquer and dominate nature but to reciprocate to nature what nature gives to man. The 'Kwan', the spirit present in each and every thing, has to be respected. A purely exploitative attitude towards nature not only spoils nature, but also the human mind.
The other Thai SHPI, the DISAC of Ubon in northeast Thailand, with its fertilizer distribution programme, pursues a somewhat different line of action. It has in common with the DISAC of Chiengmai an interest in strengthening the village economy by the promotion of rice banks, buffalo 'banks' and group savings and credit. Its philosophy has more political undertones and is somewhat less grounded in Thai traditional wisdom.

Linkages with other development agencies

Local NGOs, normally, are ready to admit that they should intensify their cooperation with each other as well as with government agencies, not for its own sake but for purely pragmatic reasons (See also Nighat Said Khan and Kamla Bhasin, 1986). There is also official recognition of the 'complementarity' of governmental and non-governmental agencies. Analysis of practice, however, shows that there is little inter-NGO collaboration and that their interrelations are coloured by discordant ideologies, conflicting objectives and personal rivalries. Relations with government institutions, too, remain highly problematic in spite of growing rapprochement between the governmental and non-governmental sectors.

MOC-Brazil over the past years has intensified its collaboration with governmental or government-controlled agencies and assists groups in getting access to development funds administered by them. The former axiom not to accept government money lest it corrupt them, is more and more abandoned in NGO circles. Apart from its intensive collaboration with some of the rural Trade Unions and APAEB, MOC deals with six more 'supporting institutions', one

70

* KAS = Konrad Adenauer Stiftung (Foundation)

genuine NGO (SIM) and five others which are government-owned or government-controlled, viz. Banco do Brasil, FUNDEC, Polonordeste, EMATER, and the Legiâo Brasileira de Assistencia.*

This last organization, for example, has an annual budget of US$ 220 million. There are many opportunities in Brazil to obtain investment credit or grants for development purposes if one knows how to find one's way through the bureaucracy. MOC sees it as its task not only to facilitate the access of self-help organizations to such facilities, but also to warn them against co-optation and manipulation by funding agencies for political ends.

The *Indonesian* study reports about six other NGOs which are operating in the Special Province of Yogyakarta, some of them very large (like Foster Parents and Dian Desa), others very small. The general picture that emerges from these NGOs described in the Indonesian study, is that they are very much 'director' dominated, have little knowledge about each other's activities, and only exceptionally collaborate with each other and government agencies. After all, contacts with government agencies would need clearance 'from Jakarta', which is a long way off. Informally, however, the village level field workers from different governmental and non-governmental agencies meet and sometimes work together. Part of the Bina Swadaya supported groups indeed did not start as UB groups but were formed earlier under the impetus of government promotion, for example as farmer groups, supported by the Ministry of Agriculture, or as PKK groups, which are women's groups operating under the supervision of the Ministry for Home Affairs, or otherwise. As such, they are good examples of complementarity of functions, which in the case of the family planning 'acceptor' groups is sanctioned by a formal agreement at Jakarta level.

Since the failed coup d'etat of 1965 and the events which followed, villagers in Indonesia are very reluctant to engage themselves in group action without the official approval of the government authorities. Typically, the term 'non-governmental organization' is in itself not officially accepted in Indonesia, since the epithet 'non-governmental' is suggestive of an anti-government stand. NGOs are therefore called LPSMs (Lembaga Pengembangan Swadaya Masyarakat, Agency for the Development of Self-Help and Self-Reliance). The official policy and practice of the Indonesian government towards NGOs is clearly expressed in an article written in 1983 by Emil Salim, Minister of State for Population and Environment: 'As long as the differences only concern problems of implementation, then the LPSMs' right to exist is guaranteed. But if differences concern... differences in ideology or in national aims, then clearly any LPSM with those sort of differences with the government will not have the right to exist' (p. 71).

---

*–SIM (Serviço de Integração de Migrantes) is an organization of Protestant origin with more or less the same objectives as MOC.

– The **Banco do Brasil** plays an important role in the implementation of a new government regulation guaranteeing minimum prices for some agricultural crops.

– FUNDEC (Fundo de Programas Cooperativos e Communitarios de Infraestrutura Rural) provides long-term, low interest loans; it aims at promoting collaboration between NGOs and GOs (Governmental Organizations).

– Polonordeste is a parastatal financing organization which enjoys World Bank support.

– EMATER is the extension-service of the Secretary of Agriculture.

– The **Legiâo Brasileira de Assistencia** is a government-sponsored, autonomous, social welfare institution, set up 40 years ago by President Vargas.

In *Thailand* the coup d'etat of 1976 caused a crackdown on development NGOs, leaving in existence only the charitable and welfare organizations. Since 1979 political conditions have changed and the NGO sector has rapidly expanded. By December 1985 the number of 'development oriented' NGOs had increased from only a few in the mid-seventies to some 200 organizations (CENDHHRA, 1985). Especially the younger NGOs are more oriented towards catalytic than entrepreneurial roles, more process than project oriented. We have seen that the strategies of the two DISACs which participated in this study, have evolved in a similar direction. Interaction between the DISACs and other NGOs not related to the Catholic Church has been limited to exchanges of information and experience at national level.*

Just as in the two other countries studied, the need for coordinated action and pooling of resources, etc., is recognized but seldom practised in field situations. The relationship between the Thai government and development NGOs is subject to rapid evolution. In 1985 the NGOs in Thailand were strongly advised to set up common platforms, both at national and regional level (north, northeast, south, and central Thailand) in order to be able to liaise coherently with the National Economic Social Development Board (NESDB). The NESDB is a government body which supervises the implementation of the five-year Development Plan (1987-1991). Such integrating moves at higher level may eventually lead to more concerted action at the lower levels. NGOs, however, are suspicious of an encroachment by government authorities upon their autonomy.

In many places, the Thai study refers to the ambiguity of feelings and practices on both sides. Government organizations have suspicions about the leftist sympathies of some NGO staff (see, for example, Tongsawate and Tips, 1985), but still want to avail themselves of NGO support for the implementation of development programmes. Both DISACs have had problems with their staff being branded as communist agents. By inviting government officials to come to their meetings and watch local development activities for themselves, the DISACs have tried to pave the way for a greater understanding between both parties. In the wake of successful NGO efforts, government administrations, too, have embarked on the promotion of rice banks and buffalo banks, while the BAAC (Bank for Agriculture and Agriculture Cooperatives) is very active in setting up credit groups in villages. But their style of intervention is quite different from that of the DISACs, as we shall see in the next section. It is the policy of the two DISACs not to duplicate government efforts or those of other development institutions, but to concentrate on the poorer villages hardly touched by government assistance. Under the new Development Plan, however, government administration intends to provide preferential assistance to those villages which so far have been neglected. This will reduce the DISACs' scope for autonomous development action and increasingly force them to organize their interventions as a reaction to what government departments and government agencies are achieving or failing to achieve. The BAAC's agressive policy of expansion in particular is at odds with the self-help promotion strategy pursued by the two DISACs.

*There is an interdenominational organization, the Centre for Religion and Development, which has been serving such a purpose since 1979.

Development dilemmas

Having reviewed the history, structure, functions and linkages of the SHPIs in the three countries, we shall now discuss some of the dilemmas the SHPIs are confronted with in their policy determination.

SHPIs act at an intermediate level and, by virtue of their position, have to seek integration in their own country in three major directions: downwards with grassroot organizations (SHOs) without falling into the trap of top-down intervention, sideways with other local NGOs, and upwards with governmental organizations, on whose political or administrative support they depend for permission to operate. In the case of Church-related organizations like the Thai DISACs, we could add as a fourth category the church administrative organs such as the Bishops' Conference or the Bishop himself. On top of these categories of organizations located in the developing country itself, we should add the funding agencies, based outside the country. All the abovementioned parties have their own interests and objectives, and must be convinced and reassured that the SHPI is pursuing a course of action which serves the common good as well as the specific interests of the party concerned. If the SHPI/local NGO fails to do so, the target population may lose interest, other NGOs may not be willing to collaborate, or the government, government-related agencies, or foreign funding agencies may stop giving their political and financial support. For the SHPIs which have participated in this study, this situation creates a series of dilemmas and constraints which have a direct bearing on the direction and nature of self-help promotion. They share these problems with many other NGOs in many other countries operating in a comparable situation.

Financial self-reliance of SHPIs
The Indonesian organization Bina Swadaya receives support from a variety of donor organizations, but one of its main funding agencies encouraged Bina Swadaya to strive for financial self-reliance by generating its own income. The SHPI had therefore engaged itself in various kinds of economic ventures – printing, book-stores, consultancy for government or international agencies, marketing – which were not directly related to its main objective: self-help among the rural poor. Within the organization the field department represents a sector of activity which is loss-making and not capable of covering its expenditure from self-earned income. Under such conditions there is a tendency to attach greater importance to the income-earning capacity of an economic activity than to its development relevance.

The SHPIs in Brazil and Thailand are in a different position. They have little or no income from own activities and are financially dependent on foreign donor contributions for the continuation of their existence. One may ask whether, for a local SHPI, there is any golden mean between self-help promotion and helping itself. This study does not attempt to answer that question, but it does illustrate the dilemma confronting local NGOs, the full dimensions of which not all donor NGOs appear to recognise.

Functional specialization
The variety of services needed by the rural poor and the urgency of the situation both push SHPIs to engage themselves in a broad range of activities, inhibiting

73

functional specialization and development of high level expertise in any one field. MOC, Brazil may serve as an example by its involvement in political work (rural trade unions), health care, organic agriculture as well as a broad range of economic activities.

Unless MOC attracts far more staff or, on a consultancy basis, draws more expertise into the process from elsewhere, it will not be able to provide high quality assistance to the 100 or so communities it serves in all four sectors of activity mentioned above. Expansion of staff is restricted not only for budgetary reasons. The present MOC staff is very much aware that expansion is likely to make the organization more bureaucratic and hierarchically structured, which in the long run is bound to affect their commitment to field work.

The conceptual framework as set out in Chapter 3 is based on the proposition that no single institution can carry the full responsibility for self-help promotion in the economic field, let alone in all sectors of development. If that statement is correct, then MOC may do well to increase its proficiency in one particular type of activity and agree to a division of tasks with like-minded NGOs (such as SIM). The idea of functional specialization between NGOs, and between NGOs on the one hand and government departments and banks on the other, may sound attractive but it assumes a willingness to share responsibilities, a coherence of objectives, and a capacity for inter-agency collaboration which are normally not there. The local NGO thus finds itself in a position where, in order to be effective, it must set priorities in the face of an ocean of unsatisfied needs and claims for its services from a huge number of people called the 'target population'.

Geographical concentration

Another dilemma closely related to the previous one results from the wide geographical areas normally covered by local NGOs. The Thai DISACs have a traditional 'constituency' of Catholic villages scattered over several provinces. The problem is exacerbated by the present preference of DISAC staff for intervention in Buddhist villages which were not associated with the DISAC's earlier welfare-oriented programmes.

At the same time there are some good arguments that geographic concentration would benefit the efficiency and effectiveness of the work: effective SHOs are not built overnight, and for them to have a real impact on processes of socio-economic change, a persistently maintained and concentrated promotional effort on a limited number of villages is necessary; inter-group and inter-village collaboration for economic purposes and the establishment of economic units at secondary level are not feasible when villages are situated at large distances from each other; each region and district has its own problems and by covering several administrative units it becomes more complicated and time-consuming to build up a system of integrated services with other non-governmental or governmental agencies.

The SHPIs in Brazil and Indonesia are in a situation which is fundamentally the same (see pp. 66-67). All this argues in favour of geographical concentration and a certain degree of functional specialization, but there are internal factors which make it difficult to implement such a policy in full. The advisory committees and boards of the SHPIs or of an organization like APAEB, comprise representatives from different provinces or districts, who will feel excluded or neglected if their regions or villages are not selected for concentrated action. It is true that the SHPIs participating in the study have already opted for a policy of concentration on existing groups, villages and districts where they operate, and that they do not envisage the expansion of their area of operation. However, for the effective promotion of economic activities and to ensure their lasting impact, a further reduction would seem necessary.

Process versus project approach
A further dilemma results from the process versus project approach discussed earlier (pp. 15-16). The dynamism and effectiveness of NGOs are judged by the amount of funds they are able to mobilize from external and internal sources, the number of projects they undertake and their demonstrable effects. This leads NGOs to be more concerned about quantity than quality, and towards a policy of what MOC researchers call 'tarefismo'. Tarefismo can be described as a no-nonsense, 'getting things done' sort of mentality, with new activities ('projects') being started without previous ones having been duly assessed on their impact and significance.

On the basis of earlier experiences the Thai DISACs have renounced such practices by giving preference to a 'quality first and quantity will follow' approach. The quality refers to the process of people becoming aware of their own situation and development potential, as a result of which they may themselves initiate economic action or otherwise. This approach contrasts with the sort of development activism manifested by most NGOs in the identification, planning and implementation of economic activities. There is the example of another DISAC which did not participate in the study. It has set up a dairy plant and a credit programme and is running a settlement scheme-cum-stock-breeding farm in a very efficient manner. Project 'beneficiaries' buy cattle feed from the DISAC, sell their products to the DISAC, and get credit and farm guidance from the same organization.

The difference between the two approaches is that in the latter case the DISAC sees it as its primary task to set up and run a service delivery system which is intended to benefit a 'client' target group. The clients are co-opted into the system as recipients. Their participation is restricted to refusal or acceptance of the service and they do not exercise any direct control over the decision-making process. This more conventional approach is capable of absorbing substantial amounts of foreign assistance. Physical outputs can be measured in terms of milk processed, credits disbursed and the number of families settled. The concrete, easily demonstrable results do not fail to impress visitors from local or international agencies. It creates grateful and dependent client-recipients, but has not much to do with self-help promotion. Nor does it stimulate the target population to think creatively and assume responsibilities beyond the narrow confines of their individual farm households. While more directive forms of intervention may be justified in an emergency situation, the pursuit of self-reliance by self-help promotion is a much slower process.

The changing roles of SHPIs
A closer study of the history of the participant SHPIs and their manner of operation shows a change of perspective and conception of roles: from 'working for the people to working with the people' (Thailand report, p. 88) and a gradual shift from executive, implementing roles as 'project holders' and 'managers' to more catalytic, supportive and sometimes protective functions. This applies to a lesser extent to the Indonesian Bina Swadaya organization: through its several

Centres it is involved in larger projects which by their nature, complexity and size are inappropriate for autonomous group action. The difference between the two approaches, the old 'service delivery' and the new 'self-help promotion', is illustrated by figure 8 below, which is a schematization. In practice one will always find a mixture of the two approaches.

Apart from the difference in structure between the two schemes, arrows in the SH promotion approach go in two directions. The double-pointed arrows illustrate the Thai 'reciprocity' concept between members and their organizations, between SHOs and a local NGO/SHPI, and between a SHPI and a foreign (or local) funding agency. Partners influence each other positively or negatively. Positive or negative change at one level is reciprocated at the other level. 'Promotion' becomes 'con-motion', for better or for worse.

Where do the SHPIs which have participated in the study stand in relation to the figure below? The two DISACs in Thailand have moved from approach 1 to approach 2 and so has MOC. The Bina Swadaya Centre for pre-cooperative development (PUSBINUB) has been close to approach 2 from the very beginning, but its other Centres apply approach 1, which offers better prospects for financial self-reliance.

Figure 8: Two different approaches in the promotion of economic activities by local NGOs

Approach 1: A service delivery approach

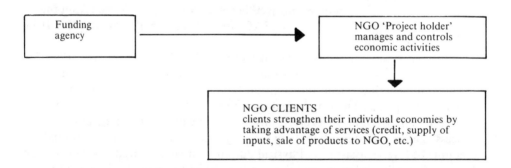

Approach 2: A self-help promotion approach

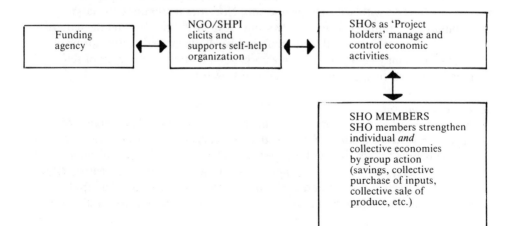

7 Self-help organizations: economic activities and performance

In this chapter we shall review the history, objectives, structure, activities, and organizational and development performance of Self-Help Organizations (SHOs), which receive support from the SHPIs discussed in the previous chapter.

APAEB - Brazil

History

MOC's involvement in the promotion of economic activities has found its most concrete expression in APAEB (Association of Small Farmers of the State of Bahia). MOC's own name, Movement for Community Organization (Movimento de Organizaçâo Comunitaria) is somewhat misleading because the 'movement' as such is embodied in APAEB and its affiliated groups, and MOC as a promoting agency has a separate statute. APAEB is the economic offshoot of a political movement which has its institutional basis in opposition groups within the 'Sindicatos', rural Trade Unions, which are supposed to guard the interests of all farmers and agricultural workers belonging to a given administrative area ('Municipio'). By government decree, trade unions were set up in the late sixties in a top-down manner and their administration was under the control of the large livestock farmers ('fazendeiros'). However, in the course of the years small farmers and labourers have increased their level of voice within these organizations, and in some cases have even succeeded in gaining control of the Trade Union administration by getting their representatives elected to the Trade Union Executive Board. Rural Trade Unions provide several services, including subsidized health càre. But where the 'progressive forces' have gained control over them, they also push for land reform, regulation of land rights by title deeds, and enforcement of an official minimum wage for agricultural workers.

APAEB had its origin in a political movement of small farmers who, by the end of the seventies, had come to realize that some sort of coordinated action at regional level was necessary to defend their interests against arbitrary decisions taken by government authorities. Such a decision was the imposition of a Value Added Tax (VAT) of 16% to be paid on all marketed produce, irrespective of the quantity. Farmers were required to register their farm enterprises and maintain records of production costs. With all documents in order, they would receive a fiscal certificate to accompany the products to the market. Small farmers were unable to fulfil such complicated and time consuming requirements and often fell victims to harassment by the police. The accumulation of fines they were forced to pay at the control posts made them lose up to 40% of the sales value of their produce.

By 1979, group leaders from different 'comunidades' and 'municipios', coordinated and assisted by MOC, decided on cooperative action. Through cooperative storage and sale of their produce, they intended to develop a system whereby the VAT would no longer be calculated and charged on the full selling price, but on the real added value. An examination of cooperative legislation by MOC revealed however that the legal provisions were too rigid, and that adoption of the cooperative statute would entail great risk of government intervention. So the groups guided by MOC opted for another legal form of enterprise: the Association. In the meantime, VAT regulations had changed. Small farmers had been exempted from payment. Nevertheless, the leaders decided to go on with the idea of forming an association, and set up a number of 'postos de venda', viz. small economic units for storage and on-sale of members' produce, and for distribution of consumer goods and agricultural implements. The more dynamic groups also started up small processing units for cassava and sisal.

In the research village, Subaé, the 'posto de venda' started in 1983. The building was constructed through 'mutirão' (traditional cooperation). The 'casa de farinha' (cassava mill) has only been in operation since 1985.

Reflecting on APAEB's history and the rapid growth of its economic activities, some APAEB spokesmen (at a workshop where the preliminary findings of the present study were discussed) voiced their opinion that the APAEB organization was in fact too much the product of MOC and a few leaders, and might have grown too fast. 'We would have done better to start with fewer people and a better prepared membership' (membership in 1980 stood at 400 and had grown to 800 in 1986). The analysis may be correct but it does not alter the fact that APAEB's creation in 1980 was the product of five years' discussion at several levels. When, in 1980, the first consumer shops were started, there was keen interest on the part of the small farmer population, which was reflected by a rapid increase in membership. The number decreased again when APAEB shops were found to be only a little cheaper than the others.

APAEB leaders and their MOC advisors had come to realize how difficult it was for APAEB, as an economic organization, to survive in a capitalist environment inimical to its fundamental goals. Closing down was out of the question, since such a failure would have meant a severe set-back for the emerging associative sector in the Feira de Santana region. Instead it was decided to broaden APAEB's economic basis and to intensify activities in the field of processing, storage and marketing of basic food items produced by its membership. As a result membership went up again to its present level.

While in many places in Brazil the Catholic Church is lending much organizational and moral support to grassroot level groups, in the Feira de Santana region this seems not to be the case. Most of the clergy have taken a conservative stand. This only adds to the authenticity of the informal, small groups out of which APAEB was born. In most cases they started as Sunday prayer groups, with religious sessions conducted by laymen for lack of a priest.

Even more outspoken criticism and opposition came from the left, viz. from the 'Pastoral Rural', a movement within the Catholic Church which supports community groups urging political and cultural reforms, but so far has given little importance to economic activities, since to undertake these might distract attention from more fundamental development aspects. This divergence of opinion on the best strategy for societal change gave rise to open conflict between APAEB and MOC on one side and Pastoral Rural on the other. At present, after a series of consultations, the relations are less strained than in the past.

APAEB objectives

In discussing APAEB objectives, it is convenient to distinguish formal from informal objectives, and to make a further differentiation between these more general objectives and the more specific ones linked to a particular form of economic activity.

The *formal* objectives of APAEB are multifarious:
– To promote cultural, educational and social activities, mutual support (mutirão), and solidarity at community level;
– To provide financial and technical assistance to its farmer membership in order to facilitate a change* in cultivation practices and to increase production;
– To promote the economic interests of its membership by providing facilities for common storage, processing and sale of members' produce, as well as by common purchase of basic consumer goods and agricultural implements for distribution to membership at cost price.
The *informal* objectives of APAEB are complementary to the formal ones, but more political in nature: to make the rural population aware of their legal rights and to get these locally recognized (especially in relation to land reform); to strengthen the claim-making capacity of its membership vis-a-vis public and semi-public organs (access to credit, seeds, etc.); to strengthen small farmers and agricultural workers in their fight to gain control over the administration and activities of the rural Trade Unions.

As an illustration of how APAEB's economically oriented objectives are being materialized we may take as an example the economic activities carried out in the research village Subaé.
The primary objective of the 'posto de venda' in Subaé is to make consumer goods and agricultural tools available at village level at the same price as in the nearby town Serrinha. Its aim, which it has in common with the other APAEB 'Postos', is to combat the ill-effects of rampant inflation. Like most other Postos, the Subaé unit has a storage and marketing section in order to be able to pay a fair price to the producers of maize, cassava flour and beans (feijâo) and to take advantage of price fluctuations. The Subaé group also runs a 'Casa de farinha' (cassava mill) which is intended to lower the costs of processing and ensure timely access to milling facilities.

79

*In documents of earlier date the word 'modernizaçâo' (modernization) was used instead of the present 'modificaçâo' (change). The change of wording is not without meaning.

Another activity is the exploitation of a collective field (Roça Comunitaria), later replaced by a collective garden (Horta Comunitaria) for horticultural production. The objective is to provide a piece of land for the landless. It should also serve as a training ground for 'Agricultura Organica', and generate income for other group activities.

APAEB structure and membership

A multi-purpose co-operative
The 'Association' APAEB operates 'de facto' as a regional multi-purpose cooperative society with branches in six small district towns (municipios) and in two more villages (comunidades), including Subaé.
Its administrative centre is at Feira de Santana, the main town in that region. The APAEB centre is situated in the same compound in which MOC has its premises. Financing has been obtained for the construction of a new building, separate from the MOC compound. The commercial centre, acting as a wholesale section for the affiliated branches, is at Serrinha, which is more centrally situated.

Legal status
The juridical situation of APAEB and its affiliated 'Postos' and processing units is somewhat ambiguous. APAEB is registered as a 'Civil Association'. Whether under present legislation a Civil Association is indeed allowed to undertake commercial activities, is a matter of interpretation. Under its present statute, APAEB still feels vulnerable to counteraction by its opponents, who may choose to combat APAEB by legal action. Because of its involvement in commerce APAEB has had to register at the Revenue Department and is subject to tax. Self-help groups consider the 'Postos' which they have built, as well as the small processing factories, as group property, but juridically, they belong to the regional organization APAEB.

The formal structure
APAEB draws its membership from six districts (municipios). Virtually all of its 800 members belong to the resource-poor category of the population (less than 10 hectares = 23 'tarefas'). Medium-size farmers (around 100 tarefas, or more) are excluded from membership for fear that they might wish to dominate the smaller ones. The landless, too, are under-represented when compared with regional figures. The regional percentage is thirty-five per cent, but their representation among APAEB membership amounts to ten only. The situation in the research village was not very different (Brazilian report, pp 85-86). The poorest households, landless and near-landless, in general cannot see any advantage in becoming an APAEB member since they have little or no agricultural produce to sell or agricultural implements to buy, and access to consumer shops is in any case free to everybody, members as well as non-members.
In order to qualify for APAEB membership a candidate must him/herself till the soil as an independent cultivator or agricultural labourer, and have no permanent employees. A strict categorization and distinction between small farmers and landless agricultural labourers depending on wage labour is not possible, as most small farmers, as in the Thai and Indonesian cases, are also part-time wage labourers.

APAEB as a regional association has a rather complex *administrative structure* (see below figure 9).

The general assembly, which is convened twice a year, is the organization's supreme body. The other organs of APAEB have recently undergone some changes (June 1986). The Administrative Council is no longer directly elected by the 800 members – many did not know for whom they were voting – but comprises all the elected members of the Branch level Directorates (Diretorias Municipais). The Chairmen of the Branch Directorates together form the General Directorate, which selects from its midst three persons to act as its Executive Committee. Prior to its recent reorganization, APAEB had an Executive Committee of twelve persons but this number was found too large for efficient work. The Executive Committee meets every month. The Administrative Council, which can be considered as a meeting of local leaders, meets every two months. There is also a small Fiscal Committee (Conselho Fiscal), which by law is responsible for the auditing of accounts and reports to the General Assembly. The Fiscal Committee at regional level is composed of the elected chairmen of the branch level Fiscal Committees.

Figure 9: APAEB structure at central level

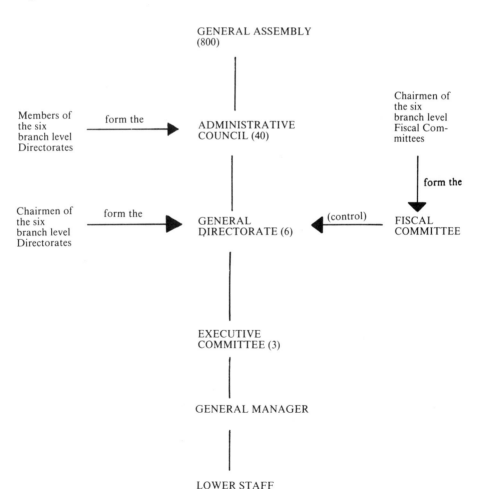

81

At the branch level (Municipio) we see a construction rather similar to the regional structure, although somewhat simpler. Each branch has an Assembly, an elected Directorate, a Fiscal Committee, a manager and various assistants. It has also certain smaller committees of three to five persons, each of them dealing with one particular activity, e.g. one for the consumer shop, one for storage, one for the processing unit, one for work at grassroot level (member education and motivation). In line with the APAEB egalitarian ideology, no Chairmen have been appointed and responsibilities have so far been shared equally among committee members. Through their participation in one or more of the Committees, about 20% of APAEB membership had to assume direct responsibility for the organizations' administration, at least officially. By a system of rotation of positions on committees and boards it was attempted to optimize such member participation. The present administrative system at branch level is still under review.

Interesting modifications in the recent administrative reshuffle were: a shift from direct election of members of the Administrative Council and APAEB Board to a system of representation by locally (branch level) elected delegates; further, the provision for a Chairman ('Presidente') to steer the work of APAEB's Executive, and the reduction of the size of the Executive Committee from 12 to 3 persons. The organisation has thus become more hierarchical, with administrative powers concentrated in the hands of fewer persons. At the same time, the democratic process has been reinforced by a streamlining of election procedures.

How it worked in practice

The problems discussed below relate to the position prior to the recent and ongoing process of restructurisation. The changes now being made, according to the action-researchers, are a direct outcome of the present study, undertaken in early 1986. Until recently a situation of 'administrative disorder' prevailed 'in which everybody is responsible for everything and, very often, nobody is responsible for anything' (Brazilian report, p. 49). The expression is somewhat tautological, but the meaning is clear.

The many roles performed by the present general manager and the ambiguity surrounding his mandate furnish part of the explanation for the muddled situation. The APAEB general manager is a person of relatively high education and skill, who undoubtedly enjoys the confidence of the Board and performs a pivotal and central role in the organization. 'If he were to leave, the whole organization might collapse' (workshop). Rather than being directed by the Board members, he is said to direct and educate them with the best of intentions. From an objective point of view, one might wonder whether it could be otherwise in a complex two-tier organization like APAEB, which serves a membership belonging to the lower strata of the rural population. In addition to being the manager, the same person is also APAEB's chief accountant. The Brazilian report explains in detail how this awkward situation has arisen (pp. 50,51). The essence is that an enterprise of the size of APAEB requires a high level of managerial skill and accountancy expertise. Such qualities are scarce and costly and do not exist within the small farmer milieu. After long discussions a solution was found by the secondment of a MOC staff member to the APAEB organization, a person trained in business accountancy and willing to perform the management and accountancy functions simultaneously. In fact, no other option was available if one takes into account the additional qualifications needed for a high level staff position in an APAEB type of organization, viz. a feeling of sympathy towards the socio-economic struggle of the small farmers, and a willingness to put oneself under the direction of a Board of small farmers in conducting the business. In short, the function requires a combination of skills and attitudes which is extremely rare in present day Brazil (and elsewhere). In view of the manager's functions and background he was bound to take up a rather dominant position in the organization, but at the same time he was conscious of the fact that it was not his task – nor would he be allowed – to take the decisions in lieu of the Executive and become APAEB's 'dono' (master). The management situation was further complicated by the ambiguous relationship between APAEB's 'centre' and the 'periphery'. No clear division of responsiblities existed between APAEB's central management and the branches where management tasks were, and still are, performed by local leaders, nor between the local managers and the various local Committees responsible for the different operations (storage, consumer shop, etc.). The spread of responsiblities over a large number of Committee members had the effect of weakening the sense of responsibility of the individual Committee member rather than provoking his active participation. Attendance at committee sessions, held twice a week, was irregular. The structure was due for reform. It is important to note, however, the catalytic role played by the present study in feeding discussions on the subject at several levels and speeding up the process of organizational change.

The situation in the research village
If we look more closely at the situation in the research village Subaé, we find APAEB activities controlled by one large family, three brothers and the wife of one of them, who also acts as branch manager. The Subaé branch counts 83 members of whom 11 are landless and 13 belong to the upper category of farmers holding 8 to 20 hectares of land. The leaders stem from this second category. According to Brazilian standards the leaders are still small farmers, but, for all that, their farming system is somewhat different from that of the really small farmers since they dedicate only a small part of their land to crop cultivation and the remainder to cattle raising. Within the APAEB Subaé group of 83, we can distinguish a more restricted sub-group of 25 members under the same leadership, which operates the 'Casa de,farinha' (cassava mill). To become a member of this more exclusive subgroup, an amount of five times the minimum daily wage has to be paid as an entrance fee (approximately US$ 6 in total) or, as an alternative, five days of work. The entrance fee is charged to compensate for the input of work by other members who have participated in the construction of the building of the mill by means of 'mutirão' (mutual help).

APAEB activities

The scheme on page 84 is an overview of the main activities carried out under the APAEB banner.

Figure 10: Overview of APAEB activities and location

Location	Activity		Posto de Venda			
	Administrative centre	Distribution centre	Consumer shop	Storage and marketing	Processing units for food crops	Collective field
Feira de Santana (m)	X	X[1]	X	planned		X
Serrinha (m)		X[2]	X	X	(maize planned)	X
Subaé (c)			X	X	cassave	X
Ichú (m)			X	X	maize	X
Valente (m)			X	X	sisal	
Araci (m)			X			X
Tanque Velho (c)			discontinued		cassave	X

m = municipio (District town)
c = comunidade (village)

1) Centre for mobile shop, serving ten other communities
2) Wholesale depot for branches

The 'Postos'
The total volume of sales of the APAEB 'Postos' together amounted in 1985 to nearly Crz. 2.5 million (US$ 182,000). From 1981 onwards, APAEB's sales have increased in real value by an annual average of 62.5%. One branch, Valente, accounts for over three-quarters of total APAEB turnover. Turnover of the other 'Postos' is small. For example, sales of the Posto of Subaé averaged Crz.650 (US$47) per day in 1985. As an annexe to the consumer section (shop) in the same building, APAEB Postos have a storage section with an average capacity of 700 to 800 bags (4 to 5 tons). Cassava flour, maize flour and beans are bought from members who receive the current day's price when delivering their produce to the Posto. Some of the farmers' produce is sold through the consumer shop, but the greater part is kept in store to be sold at a higher price to middlemen or government bodies when market prices have risen.

The substantial increase in turnover of APAEB can be attributed mainly to the consumer section, especially the one at Valente. The Valente Posto sells consumer articles and agricultural implements at near-cost price, the consequence of which we shall review below when discussing APAEB's financial performance.

The consumer sections of the Postos have a large assortment of 450 different articles. Available information did not permit differentiation between slow and fast moving consumer items, but it seems safe to say that a great part of the assortment fills up the shelves without adding much to the volume of the Postos' business.

Processing units
The 'Casa de farinha' (cassava mill) in the research village Subaé is a medium-size mill which has a capacity of some ten bags per day (during 11 to 12 hours of operation; one bag is 60 kg). Its capacity is twice that of the smaller traditional mills, which is an advantage during the main harvest season (three months in the year), but it is only one third of that of the much larger and more 'modern' one at Tanque Velho. The capacity of the latter is generally considered too large, since

the group is unable to use it to its full capacity. Bottlenecks are the scraping by hand (cassava has to be scraped before milling) and transport of produce to and from the cassava mill. The cassava mill at Subaé is much more economical, especially compared with traditional milling practice. Energy consumption (firewood and gasoline) is much lower, which brings considerable benefit to its users (for details see 'Economic impact').

The other APAEB processing units, such as the threshing mill for maize at Ichu and the sisal processing unit at Valente ('Batadeira'), have not been studied in detail, owing to lack of time. The overall situation, however, is that the APAEB branches (postos) and the processing units do not work on full capacity. The major problem is a lack of working capital ('capital de giro'), which is more difficult to obtain from funding agencies than credits or grants for investment purposes. The amount of available working capital is further reduced by the sale of consumer goods on credit terms.

Collective fields

The collective field (roça comunitaria) in the research village has not been a success: according to the villagers the idea had come mainly from outsiders (MOC). The selected field was abandoned but the idea was maintained. The group decided to start up a common garden for horticultural production and through MOC received a small loan, a cistern and a pump. Unfortunately, the irrigation system did not work as well as expected and the project was temporarily discontinued. Members intend to re-start it shortly, once the technical problems have been solved. In other localities collective fields are said to be doing better.

Mobile shop

Recently a new activity was started by the APAEB wholesale centre, the so-called 'Posto volante' or mobile shop. It serves ten 'comunidades' (villages), where it sells consumer articles and purchases farm products direct from the farmers. The assortment is limited to fifty articles only. The first experiences show high interest on the part of the rural public. The 'Posto volante' buys from, and sells to, all the villagers. A great part of the trade is done by barter: the small producer brings his products and gets the monetary equivalent in consumer goods.

APAEB organizational performance

Financial autonomy

What emerges from the MOC study as a general conclusion is that APAEB is still far from having achieved financial autonomy, a situation which makes the whole organization vulnerable and dependent on cheap loans for investment, and on grants from foreign agencies.

In 1985, APAEB still had a positive cash-flow. This was due to donor gifts being used to meet current expenditure, and also to some financial speculation.* If such gifts had not existed and if depreciation of assets is taken into account, APAEB's

*Speculating on the short-term money market was common practice in Brazil until the monetary reform of 28th February 1986, aimed at stopping the galloping inflation.

deficit on its 1985 business can be estimated at Crz 366,000 (US$ 26,600) which amounts to 14.6% of its sales. Donor contributions, directed at meeting current expenditure, have in fact in the past obscured perception as to the economic viability of the economic undertakings and their capacity for self-sustenance. The above deficit figure does not take into consideration the received 'subsidios nâo-contabilizados' or 'hidden' subsidies, mainly interest subsidies (84%), which are received in the form of interest-free investment loans or grants from local parastatal bodies or donor agencies. A minor part of the hidden subsidies (16%) consists of direct salary payments by MOC to some of the APAEB staff.

Taking hidden subsidies into account – which in fact must be done if one wishes to assess how far APAEB is from 'financial autonomy' as defined in Chapter 3 – the negative figure over 1985 would increase by an additional Crz 347,000 (US$ 25,000) (Brazilian report, p. 64). However, there is some justification for leaving out some of these hidden subsidies in cost calculation. Interest subsidies and investment grants could be looked upon as investments of an infrastructural nature, especially when they concern an upcoming business which will benefit small farmers in an economically disadvantaged rural area. But costs of depreciation of capital goods certainly must be taken into account and incorporated in profit and loss statements.

The above findings are disturbing, but there are also some positive signs which have resulted from a more detailed investigation of individual units. The deficits stem from the larger units such as the Posto de Valente, its sisal processing unit and the large Casa de Farinha (cassava mill) at Tanque Velho. The smaller Posto and cassava mill at Subaé, however, have succeeded in breaking even, if we accept the premise that during the 'take-off' period it is acceptable not to take the above mentioned 'hidden subsidies' into consideration for cost calculation.

Lack of working capital (not to be confused with subsidies to cover current expenditure) constitutes another handicap in developing the more profitable storage and marketing section. The dearth of working capital means that Postos are forced to sell members' produce to third parties at a time when prices are not particularly attractive. Some financial agencies, both international and national ones (like Polonordeste), are reluctant or unwilling to provide working capital. This is an external factor which cannot be changed easily. Such reluctance also has some justification. If we take the APAEB situation as a case in point, working capital contributions are likely to be converted into subsidies to make up for operating losses. The shortage of liquid resources is exacerbated by an internal factor: the reduction of the available working capital by the sale of consumer goods on credit to APAEB membership. The study was not able to assess precisely the effect of credit operations on APAEB's liquidity position, but there are instances where, at Posto level, outstanding debts with members amounted to twice the monthly turnover.

According to earlier APAEB records of the six branches/postos, three are in surplus, and three others loss-making. But on the basis of the present study we may say that, according to normal standards of accountancy, the 'resultado positivo' of the surplus-making branches cannot be considered really positive since depreciation of assets and other direct subsidies were not considered. An effort has been made to calculate the volume of turnover at which APAEB would break even, if donor gifts for covering operational costs were to cease, and taking depreciation into account. The calculation was necessarily tentative, since the prevailing bookkeeping system does not allow a clear distinction between variable and fixed costs. If we follow the action-researchers' estimate that one third of APAEB's present costs are variable and vary proportionally with turnover, there is no prospect whatsoever of a positive result since the gross profit margin (5%) just equals the variable costs (calculations based on data given on p. 60 of the Brazilian report). If we take both the present level of costs and the gross profit margin as fixed, APAEB would need a volume of sales six times higher than the present one for a positive cash-flow.

In the APAEB case there is still urgent need for an even more profound economic analysis than could be done under the present study. Such an analysis should assess the prospects of economic viability of each of the separate economic units operating under the APAEB umbrella. This can be done only on the basis of an adjusted system of cost-accounting, which gives more precise information on the nature of costs (fixed or variable) and permits their allocation to each Posto and each section within the Posto, e.g. a differentiation between costs to be allocated to the consumer and storage sections respectively. On the basis of this information and a complementary marketing study, new policies will have to be devised in relation to pricing, sale of consumer goods on credit terms (if this is to be permitted at all), expansion or reduction of the enterprise, taking into account both the social and economic consequences of all these decisions.

In assessing the present financial performance of APAEB it should be realized that consumer shops in rural areas have proved to be one of the most difficult cooperative type of enterprises to run on a profitable basis because of: pressure from membership for consumer goods to be sold on credit terms; relatively high transport costs; competition from small dealers and the attraction of towns for rural people who like to go on a shopping spree. All this applies in full to the APAEB situation whose Postos are situated at large distances from each other (on average 70 kms).

If sufficient working capital were made available, APAEB might be able to compensate its losses in the consumer sector through greater surpluses from the storage and sale of staple food crops. Its processing activities, if conducted on a small scale, might generate additional revenue, while the mobile shop might help to boost sales without adding too much to overhead costs.

Administrative and managerial autonomy
During the early eighties there were tensions between the APAEB 'centre' and the APAEB 'periphery'. The Committees of the Postos and branch managers accused the 'centre', advised by MOC, of imposing management systems and practices. The Postos claimed and obtained greater administrative and managerial autonomy. MOC staff deliberately started keeping themselves at a greater distance from the APAEB decision-making processes. This proved to be a useful learning experience for both parties, which eventually resulted in a greater convergence of ideas on price and credit policies.

APAEB has achieved a high degree of administrative and managerial autonomy in spite of its short existence and the relative complexity of its affairs. But as we have seen, its managerial autonomy at the central level has a *weak* basis in the form of a *strong* general manager.

Of late, the salary of the general manager has been fully borne by APAEB. This will also help correct the asymmetry of the relationship between the Executive Committee and the general manager.

Participation
In terms of member participation the Brazilian report distinguishes three categories. Those who participate in discussions on policy and organization of activities; those whose participation is restricted to frequent use of facilities; those who make little use of services and show poor interest in general. The most active group is the smallest. According to the leaders themselves (source of information: local workshop), the great majority of APAEB membership view the organization as belonging to its protagonists, that is to say the leaders, whom they know to be supported by MOC. Meanwhile, the leaders complain of being heavily occupied by administrative and supervisory tasks which leave them no time for educational and motivational work. While even the leaders have difficulty in fully understanding the ever increasing complexity of APAEB business, this is even more true of the ordinary member who is less educated, more often than not illiterate, and too much occupied by his (her) everyday struggle for subsistence. Leaders' or other members' work for APAEB is compensated by an amount of money corresponding to the official daily minimum wage (approx. US$ 2).
In the research village, the Directorate of the Posto decided to distribute part of the (fake) surplus of the 1985 operations among the membership according to two criteria: regularity and volume of purchases by the members from the consumer shops; attendance at meetings. On this basis members were categorized into five groups. The highest category received 100 Crz (approx. US$ 8) and the lowest nothing. The list of names showing the category in which each of them had been placed was put on display outside the shop and caused some frustration among part of the membership who felt underrated.

For an outsider it is very difficult, if not impossible, to judge whether the benefits of a cooperatively undertaken activity are being distributed among membership in an equitable manner. As we shall see further on, easy and timely access to a co-operative service such as the milling facility offered by the 'Casa de farinha', is economically of much greater importance than the small amounts members may receive from sharing in the 'surplus' of the Posto.
Certainly a positive mark is the fact that APAEB leaders themselves judge a higher degree of member participation to be highly desirable in every respect and meriting special promotional effort.

APAEB development performance

Economic impact
–The consumer shop
The prices APAEB members and non-members have to pay for consumer articles sold by the Posto in Subaé village, are more or less equal to those they would have to pay in the nearby district town, Serrinha. Before the Posto started, the small shops at Subaé charged prices three times higher. Now most of the small shops have closed or brought down their prices considerably.* Moreover, by

---

* The Postos based in town, like those in the villages, have forced private merchants to lower their retail selling prices to consumers and raise their buying prices from producers for cassava flour, maize and beans. With regard to the important donor-financed deficits of the town-based Postos, it seems legitimate to express some doubt about the fairness of such competition on the part of APAEB. It was not possible to study this issue since the focus of the research was rural.

buying at the Posto, villagers save time (half a day a week) and transport costs to the district town. The saving can be calculated at Crz 40 (approx. US$3) per trip. These aspects, transport and time, are particularly important for that section of the population which is least mobile (the women in general and the poorer families) and which can least afford to sacrifice half a day for shopping purposes. By reducing the number of trips to town from 52 to 13, the household may save up to Crz 1,560 (approx. US$ 113) a year or approximately 10% of its income (figures based on household surveys, pp. 106/107, Brazilian report). It should be borne in mind, however, that most of the APAEB Postos are not located in villages but in small district towns where they have to face fierce competition from many private small and large shop owners. In the latter case the positive effects on members' income and time budget do not seem to be very important. Subaé, in this respect, is thus to be regarded as a particular case in point, not representative of APAEB as a whole.

–Storage and marketing
The impact of the food crops storage and marketing section of the Subaé Posto was also hard to assess. APAEB buys its members' marketable surplus of processed food crops (cassava flour, maize flour, beans) at the current market price. This price varies day by day. But due to lack of working capital APAEB can afford to buy only a small part of the members' production (estimated at 5 to 10%). Thus the APAEB objective of providing a secure outlet for members' products has so far been fulfilled only to a limited extent. By delivering their products to the village Posto instead of having to transport their cassava flour, beans or maize flour to the town market, members save considerably on transport costs. Transport costs to town average 25% of the selling price. For the households covered by the household survey the potential yearly benefit was calculated at Crz 151 (US$ 11) per household. However, since households had been able to sell only a part of their marketed produce to APAEB, the actual benefit was much less.
Another effect of a storage and marketing facility at village level is a shortening of the commercial circuit. The same basic food items, bought from the farmers, are sold through the consumer shop to the people living in Subaé or its immediate neighbourhood. Priority is given to sales to villagers, only the remainder being sold in bulk to outsiders. The beans and flour, as well as the seeds, are stored in zinc containers without the use of any chemicals for conservation. Treatment is based on a traditional method of food and seed conservation and works perfectly well.

–Seed distribution and agricultural extension
APAEB also distributes seeds for food crops to counteract the 'sementes de meia' system, under which the producer has to cede half the harvest to the person who has provided the seed. By acquiring a stock of seed from government bodies, APAEB thus ensures that its small farmer membership get their legitimate share of state subsidy programmes. Seed distribution is complemented by the APAEB/ MOC extension programme of 'agricultura organica'. Fifteen farmers in Subaé have changed from chemical to organic fertilizers. By using a plough, the same farmers have been able to extend, often double, their planted area without resorting to tractor hire services. Farmers' leaders however admitted that the somewhat better-off categories among APAEB membership are the main beneficiaries of the APAEB/MOC agricultural extension programme.

–Cassava milling

Farmers of Subaé who happen to be members of the cassava mill sub-group (25 out of 83 APAEB members), derive considerable benefit from using the group's milling facilities. Action-researchers calculated a net gain of Crz 38 (nearly US$ 3) per bag (equivalent to one and a half times the minimum daily wage).*

For the average member household in Subaé producing 16 to 17 bags per year, the net gain can be calculated at about Crz 640 per household (US$ 46, Brazilian report, p. 104).**

The price of cassava flour is subject to considerable fluctuations, but still on average remains so low that cassava production for the market is a loss-making activity if labour input is calculated at the minimum daily rate. But farmers continue to grow it since it is a food crop. The increased milling capacity of the Subaé group also helps to 'save the manioc' ('salva de manioca'). Saving of the manioc is important when the harvest risks being lost because of heavy rains.

We have seen earlier that the entrance fee for becoming a member of the cassava mill group is relatively high (5 times the minimum daily wage or approximately US$ 10), but still very reasonable when compared with the expected benefit of about US$46 for the average household.

The combined effect of the APAEB economic activities on the situation of its member households is very hard to assess. The short existence of APAEB economic units in the research village, the sample size and the nature of the information collected, do not allow the drawing of firm conclusions in terms of increased income for specific categories of APAEB membership. Yet from the available qualitative and quantitative information and approximate calculations based on the above, it became clear that:

– The average Subaé household in a position to take full advantage of the various facilities APAEB offers – and until now, it should be recognized, few of them are in such a position – may save about $ 150 a year (or 13% of its income). This benefit is derived not so much from producing more, but from having to pay less for consumer goods, for agricultural implements, storage and marketing facilities. Even taking into account the small operational deficits of some of these village-based activities, the analysis still confirms the potential of cooperative forms of action in rationalizing the local economy for the benefit of those who need such change most, the small farmers and landless families.

– APAEB activities cover only part of the broad range of economic activities of farm households. APAEB storage, marketing and processing are mainly geared to crop growers, but most of the member and non-member households' cash income was found to stem from stockbreeding and raising, and off-farm employment. In other words, the potential seems not to be tapped to the full, yet.

– Direct contact with families also made action-researchers aware that in the determination of economic activities, the specific situation of women and rural youth had not been taken into account. From a village perspective it can be

90

---

*The minimum daily wage in March 1986 amounted to Crz 25 per day (approx. US$ 2).
**The amount was calculated on the basis of a market price of Crz 60 (!) per bag. The difference between group milling and traditional milling fluctuated with the market price because part of the rent of the mill is paid in cassava flour (10 ltrs per bag).

concluded that the economic benefits are unequally spread over the target population. First, one third of village households are not APAEB members and visit the consumer shop irregularly; secondly, priority of access to cassava milling facilities is given to the members of the small sub-group. Non-members can get their cassava milled only by paying a 60% higher rent as a milling fee.

In the case of Subaé village, it was found that, even though the self-help idea has gained some momentum, an important part of the target population still remains indifferent to APAEB and participates only marginally in SHO activities. For the more active the emerging associative sector so far covers only part of the household economy. Since the situation in other 'comunidades' supported by MOC is no more advanced, MOC action-researchers concluded that, with the possible exception of a few households, the 'economic projects' have not yet been able to arrest the process of growing poverty in the localities serviced by MOC. For the moment they have succeeded only in slowing it down. But for the future there is still ample scope for economic activities to expand and acquire greater significance, provided they succeed in attracting greater participation from membership in the executive tasks.

Social, political, and cultural impact
The economic activities so far have produced very little change in power relationships within the village of Subaé. Those village leaders who are actively involved in APAEB activities have strengthened their position vis-à-vis leaders who are not. When the conservative mayor makes his speeches, villagers now dare to raise critical questions. In other places too, according to the workshop participants, APAEB activities have heightened the leaders' sense of responsibility and morality, while ordinary APAEB members, by belonging to a group, also feel more secure.

The Postos have become important meeting points for informal chats or more serious discussions. 'Mutirão', mutual help, is regaining importance. Group leaders feel more confident and have started addressing themselves directly to public or semi-public authorities based in the provincial or district capitals, to demand better service. APAEB leaders are now considering setting up at Subaé level a specific section of the rural Trade Union, which would strengthen the capacity of its Subaé members to influence decision-making at regional level. Women's participation in APAEB-led discussions and activities is still poor. Yet APAEB has recently started putting into practice the 'equal pay for equal work' principle, which is exceptional in a cultural setting where men are normally paid two to three times more than women for the same work. (Brazilian report, p. 110) The Brazilian case study is a good illustration of the complexity of impact assessment. What matters most in human development, such as increased self-confidence, creative capacity and social concern, is the most difficult to measure.

Summary of APAEB performance
The financial performance of APAEB as a whole is very poor. The town-based **91** Postos and the larger processing units for agricultural produce have made heavy losses. Smaller selling points and processing units, such as in the research village Subaé, are doing much better financially and indications are that they also have a much greater impact on the processes of economic, social and political change. If APAEB is to become independent from donor grants for its normal operations, then the ongoing administrative re-structurisation of APAEB will have to be

followed by an economic re-structurisation, giving priority to the multiplication of small village-based economic units over the larger town-based ones.

Usaha Bersama – Indonesia

History of UBs

The movement of 'Usaha Bersama' (Indonesian for 'joint efforts') was initiated in the fifties by the Pancasila Farmers Union (Ikatan Petani Pancasila). It has found its most concrete expression through the formation of small cooperative units, called UBs, with savings and credit as their main activity. Some 400 UBs spread over Java and South Sumatra receive guidance from Bina Swadaya, but the UB system of administration of savings and loans is extended to many other places in Indonesia.

UB groups are normally grafted upon already existing indigenous groups, such as 'arisan' (a traditional savings club), PKK groups (government promoted women's groups), or male farmers' groups (promoted by the Extension Department). Such groups have become UB groups by adopting the UB system, but they all have very much their own individual history.

The 7 UB groups operating in the selected research area (Gunung Kidul district, Yogyakarta Special Province) were founded between 1968 and 1970. The close ties between the UB movement in its early days and the Catholic church are reflected in the UB membership of the older units. Groups of later date have a more mixed membership and comprise many persons registered as Moslem, as in the case of the young farmers' group in the second research village, Pacing, which is 85% Islamic.

UB objectives

The main official long-term objectives of the UB are to support the undertaking of economic activities by its membership and to foster community solidarity. To reach such objectives UBs have concentrated on the provision of credit facilities to members for productive purposes, and the pooling of savings for capital formation.

Such are the formal, organizational objectives. We shall see hereafter that, informally, UB members may pursue objectives which are quite different from those officially pursued by the UB organization.

UB structure

92

UB groups count on average 40 members. The average for the 7 groups in the two research villages is 36. According to the action-researchers, group size is likely to remain at the same level for the following reasons: some groups have a membership restricted to a special professional category like teachers and technical staff of a particular school; some identify themselves with a particular religion (Catholic); UB groups with a more affluent membership tend to shut out the poorer members of the community; finally, there is competition for members from many other official and semi-official groups in the villages (see Chapter 5), each of them asking for some form of monetary contribution.

Of the seven UB groups in the two research locations, one is a women-only group of 58 persons. In the other six UBs, women constitute a small (below one third) or even tiny minority.

Members in the first research location, Baleharjo, belong predominantly to the better-off sections of the population: teachers, traders, government officials, who mostly have more than one source of income. Many UB members have engaged themselves in money-lending, but would normally avoid doing so in their own villages, where they carry on one or more of the abovementioned professional occupations. In the research locations, money-lending did not appear to be regarded as morally objectionable behaviour. The borrower considers the lender 'as a very good person because when I need rice I can get the rice or the money to buy it'. The service is welcomed, even if the rate is high (up to 25% per month). In the second research village, Pacing, members were all farmers, male or female. They were selected by the group leader, in conjunction with the extension officer, on the basis of their dynamism and their potential for agricultural production (they possess more land and livestock than the average farmer).

The board of UBs can be small (3) or large (17), involving half the membership. Functions rotate every second year, but normally among the same persons. UBs have the status of a 'pre-cooperative'. Official cooperative status is reserved for the government controlled KUDs (Koperasi Unit Desa), which operate at sub-district level. By law KUDs were given the monopoly of cooperative activities in rural areas but, in fact, there is room for self-help and similar sorts of groupings to carry on economic activities on their own as long as they do not hinder the operation of the KUDs.

UB activities

The savings and loan business is the main economic activity of the UB groups. Where they are involved in other productive or trade activities, this is viewed by the membership as a supplementary activity. All seven groups in the research villages have benefited from the Bina Swadaya managed solidarity credit programme KSK, but not all take loans every year (KSK credit is normally given for one year).*

–Credit
Elsewhere in Indonesia the KSK programme is steadily expanding, but in the research villages, groups seem to have reached the upper limit of their credit absorption capacity.

For the year 1985, the total figure for the seven groups stood at Rp 28 million (US$ 25,000), which was about 15% less than two years earlier. Groups charge 3% to 4% per month to their borrowers and pay a monthly 2% interest rate to

93

*For more information on the KSK programme, see Chapter 6, p. 69 and Chapter 8, p. 114.

Bina Swadaya. Three UB groups have received additional credit from BS for investment in collective economic production. The interest rate charged for such a purpose is lower: 1.5%. The term of repayment is 3 years.

–Multivarious use of loans
Loans to members are officially given for productive purposes. From interviews with members, it was learned that loans are used for a variety of purposes, such as payment of school fees, hospital bills, etc., and only occasionally for financing trade or investment. The average size of (short-term) loans to members is considerable by local standards, varying between Rp 14,500 (US$ 13.8) to Rp 285,000 (US$ 253)! Default is rare.

–Savings
All groups save. Members have to pay an entrance fee of between Rp 1,000 and Rp 5,000 (approx. US$ 1 to 4), and are obliged to save regularly an amount of Rp 500 to Rp 1,000 per month (approx. US$ 0.5 to 1), on which no interest is paid. Two out of the seven groups pay 4% interest to members on voluntary savings. By the end of 1985 total savings per group varied between Rp 750,000 and Rp 2,270,200 (US$ 660 to 2,000). On top of this, groups contribute to the Bina Swadaya 'solidarity fund' in order to get access to the KSK credit programme. Their contributions range from Rp 67,000 to Rp 1,350,000 per group (US$ 60 to 1,200).

–UB economic activities
The overview of the economic activities conducted by the UB groups (Figure 11) shows a high rate of failure.

UB groups apparently have difficulty in initiating and conducting economic activities on a profitable basis, while for individual economic activities members get little support other than credit. Interest and ideas are there but management capabilities are lacking both at group and individual level.

Organizational performance

Financial, administrative and managerial autonomy
The most remarkable achievement of the UB groups is that all are making a surplus on their savings and loan transactions. A margin of 2 to 3 % between credit and saving interest rates is more than enough to cover their administrative costs. Default is very rare. The sense of obligation and discipline are high, both of members towards their UB and of the UB groups vis-à-vis the BS organization. The latter acts as a cheap finance house for UB credit operations.
The overall picture emerging from the analysis of economic activities is that in this respect, UB groups are still passing through a learning phase of trial and error, with failures exceeding successes. When reviewing the use of instruments of self-help promotion later in this report we shall discuss the need of UBs for consultancy services (Chapter 8).
The UB groups operate as autonomous units. They administer and manage their own affairs. Bookkeeping for loan and savings transactions in general is well maintained, but recording in respect of economic productive activities is poor or

Figure 11: Overview of UB economic activities in both research locations

Activity ('Project')	UB groups 1 to 7	Investment in R$_p$ (US$)	Result
1. Winged bean	UB group no. 1	1,000,000 ($ 890)	Some members used credit given for winged bean production for other purposes, those who produced winged beans faced a loss Processing by local NGO (Dian Desa) was stopped due to marketing problems, so was the UB 'project'
2. Rice hulling production and marketing	UB group no. 1 and no. 3	10,000,000 ($8900)	Poor management, confusion about ownership of rice brought to the huller; poor bookkeeping: huller was used by chairman for personal profit, hulling was stopped at the end of year of operations; project is being reconsidered
3. Winged bean production and marketing	UB group no. 3	300,000 ($ 266)	Discontinued for same reasons as project no. 1 (see above)
4. Goat raising	UB group no. 3	110,000 ($ 100)	Small surplus after 6 months of operations, if labour impact is not counted; later in 1985 discontinued because of losses
5. Fish pond	UB group no. 3	17,000 ($ 15)	All fish vanished during flood
6. Food crop	UB group no. 3	750,000 ($ 670)	Net profit of R$_p$ 153,600 ($ 135) in one year from purchase and sale of maize and soya beans
7. Incubator	UB group no. 3	Grant from extension department	Incubator never worked
8. Consumer shop	UB group no. 2	100,000 ($ 89)	Small surplus, low turnover, sales only to schoolteachers and other school staff; members show little interest
9. Cow fattening	UB group no. 1	2,810,000 ($ 2,500)	Investment is spread over 3 years; small surplus if labour impact is not counted
10. Horticulture	UB group no. 7	Labour only	Cultivation of vegetables (onions, garlic) proved very profitable; this helped to build up the UB group's capital fund
11. Krupuk factory	UB group no. 7	1,100,000 ($ 980)	Financial result difficult to assess because of absence of bookkeeping system; factory was started in October 1985 at the wrong time (beginning of rainy season)

absent. This makes it impossible for either Bina Swadaya supporting staff or UB leaders and membership to get a clear insight into the profitability of the collective undertakings.

Participation
Attendance at monthly meetings is high and regular in the four 'active groups', less so in the three more 'passive groups' (p. 67, Indonesian report). Monthly meetings are normally used to disburse credits and receive deposits. The group 'leader' acts as the 'group engine'. It depends primarily on the leader's initiative and managerial capabilities whether meetings are actually held and used to discuss the undertaking of new or ongoing economic activities. Discontent with leadership on the part of membership is seldom expressed openly or verbally during meetings, but is made apparent by members refraining from attendance.

Development performance

Socio-economic impact
One of the reasons why the present study had to expand to a second village cluster, Pacing, was that in the one first selected, Baleharjo, UB membership was found to be concentrated within the better-off sections of the population with a per capita income of more than twice that of non-members.*
But in the case of Pacing, too the UB membership was found to be composed of 'progressive', young, and relatively well-to-do farmers. As set out in Chapter 1, the Pacing UB members can nevertheless be considered as belonging to the rural poor given the low living standard of the village as a whole. This finding, the concentration of UB membership among the more well-to-do section of the village population, is quite consistent with those of other studies on UB cases (see Bina Desa study, 1985). It is also more or less commonly known among field workers (local workshop, December 1985) and it calls for a review of Bina Swadaya promotional practice if the organization is to meet its declared objectives.

The raison d'être of a UB group from the members' point of view
Leaders and relatively rich UB members with a yearly household income of between $ 2,000 and $ 4,000 were found – as appeared from household surveys and follow-up discussions – not to need the UB facilities as such for access to cheap credit. They already have access to, and receive credit from, other informal village groups or official credit institutions like the BRI (Bank Rakyat Indonesia) or the KUDs (p. 77, Indonesian report). For leaders, UB groups are economically insignificant, but they have an important social function by confirming their leadership position.

For the average UB member – who in a village perspective belongs to the middle-income section – UB membership has several advantages. First of all, it affords prestige. All the members interviewed stated that their status in the village had increased due to their UB membership. The poorer the member, the prouder he

96

---

*For details, see Indonesian report, p. 75.

or she is to belong to a UB group which through its participation in the KSK programme is able to provide larger loans than can be obtained elsewhere.* The contracting of a large loan is a symbol of trust, and for that reason is appreciated and might be taken even if the borrower had no immediate need for cash. Secondly, in cases where members need the cash, credit is normally used for such purposes as housing, education, consumption, etc.. It is highly valued because even for a middle-income household it is hard to find credit at a moderate rate from other sources (money-lenders may charge 25% per month). In the UB groups based on neighbourhood (and not on occupation, such as teachers), some members were found to belong to poor households. For them the obligatory monthly saving, the payment of interest and repayment obligations can become a real burden. But to withdraw from UB membership would mean a loss of face, which he or she would want to avoid at any price. As a matter of fact, one local UB leader in Baleharjo, who through the participation of his UB in the present study became much more aware of this type of contradiction, arrived at the conclusion that the poorer members of the community need their own UB groups. Such economicallly more homogeneous groups would be more appropriate to the specific savings and credit needs of the poorer sections of the population. The leader regarded it as his personal duty to motivate and assist the poorer villagers to get their own groups started in the coming years.**

From the above we can see that the villagers have their own criteria for utility assessment and impact, which may differ considerably from those applied and perceived by development agencies.
In trying to assess the impact of UB groups on the village and household economy one should take into account the high level of income derived by households from non-farming activities in the Gunung Kidul District villages. Even in the second research village, from the outside a village whose economy and social life is primarily based on agriculture, only one out of the five households investigated was found to earn over 50% of its income from agricultural occupations. Considering the political impact, we may conclude that in the research localities the existence of UBgroups has not led to any change towards a more egalitarian society. Such is not the objective of its leadership, nor is it regarded as a feasible proposition by the 'target population'. The Indonesian study concludes that 'if the trends shown can be verified through studies on a wider scale and with as larger sample, the UB system is still far removed from the poorest of the poor who are the millionfold quoted target group of all SHPIs' (Indonesian report, p. 79).

97

---

*All interviewed UB group members stated that their status in the village had increased due to their UB membership.
**The assessment of the situation by this UB leader is probably correct. Although the number of socio-economic groups existing in Baleharjo is already excessively high, low income households were found to participate in only a very few groups, membership of which was almost compulsory, such as the 'village security group' or the PKK groups (women's groups).

Self-help groups in Thailand

History

A comparison between the two Thai research villages shows quite different histories of self-help organisation.

In Ban Isan, the first organisation to be set up was a small Credit Union of 16 members. This was in 1973. Since then this 'core group' has received a lot of material, technical and moral support from DISAC Ubon. This has enabled membership to rise to 73 persons and to broaden the range of activities. In 1979, a rice bank and fertilizer programme were started with financial and technical support from DISAC. Subsequently, the SHO received further support from government sources for a 'buffalo bank' and the enlargement of the existing rice bank. More recently, the SHO has also started a medicine bank and begun the collective purchase of basic consumer goods. The group's development can be summarized as follows:

1973	Credit Union	DISAC support
1977	Rice 'Bank'	DISAC support B 20,000, and additional Government support B 60,000
1979	Buffalo 'Bank'	Government support, approx. B 50,000
1980	Fertilizer 'Bank'	DISAC support B 60,000 (estimated)
1985	Collective purchase of consumer goods	Self-financed and government support
1985	Medicine 'Bank' and improved sanitation (latrines, sewage disposal)	Self-financed

All the activities started since 1973 have continued up to the present day.

What makes a comparison with the other village, Ban Nua, so interesting is that the SH movement in Ban Nua started spontaneously without any outside catalytic intervention. It was only in 1982, having heard about DISAC's buffalo bank scheme, that the Buddhist village leaders decided to enter into an agreement for collaboration with DISAC. Since then the number of self-help groups in Ban Nua village has rapidly expanded while the older groups, number 1 and 2, have taken on new economic and social functions. Schematically, the development of the groups in Ban Nua can be presented as follows:

1975	Consumer shop of Group no. 1	No outside support; activity was stopped; results were disappointing
1976/77	Rice Bank of Group no. 1	No outside support; initially failed, then succeeded
1977	Rice Bank of Group no. 2	No outside support
1983/84	Five more Rice Banks by five new groups, including two belonging to landless labourers	Mutual support between village groups (rice donations). DISAC provided only catalytic support
1985	Women's group for pig raising	Self-financed

All activities started since 76/77 have continued up to the present day.

Comparing the two approaches, we see that the rice bank in Ban Isan was started with DISAC's material support, but the eight much smaller rice banks, grouping 10 to 12 people, in Ban Nua received no external material assistance. In Ban Nua members of the first two groups to be created, belonged to the more affluent section of the population. They later contributed to the formation of rice 'capital' for the poorer groups. The contribution was materialized during a traditional rice giving ceremony (Thod Pha Pa Kao ceremony) paying tribute to the spirit of the rice ('Kwan'). The two groups created last had a membership which was predominantly landless. The assistance of the DISAC Chiengmai apparently facilitated the 'trickle-down' of the 'group formation' idea from the more affluent to the poorer sections of the community.

The rice banks in the two villages, Ban Isan and Ban Nua, were started in the same period after a country-wide period of drought. Subsequently, during the late seventies and early eighties, the groups and the self-help movement in the two villages developed their own momentum. Not mentioned above is that all the small self-help groups in Ban Nua have started saving schemes.

In the two villages the groups have claimed and received support from different agencies, governmental and non-governmental. The buffalo bank in Ban Isan was started with government support (a gift), in Ban Nua with DISAC support (a loan). Ban Isan also participated in a fertilizer distribution programme managed by the DISAC of Ubon. The progamme was meant to assist DISAC-supported groups in getting access to subsidized fertilizer distributed by a parastatal organization. But groups 1 and 2 in the other village, Ban Nua, received fertilizer on credit from the government-controlled BAAC (Bank for Agriculture and Agricultural Cooperation) without any DISAC intervention.

It is important to note, too, that in neither of the two villages did the SH movement start among the poorer half of the village population but among the relatively well-to-do sections of the farming population. Further, the SHOs in both villages have succeeded in maintaining their autonomy in spite of the acceptance of support from government or government-controlled organizations. The Thai report describes in greater detail how relations with such bodies occasionally became very tense when the latter, without success, tried to impose their rules and regulations upon the SHOs as a condition for the release of government grants or access to other facilities.

Objectives

The objective of the rice bank is to ensure for its membership access to rice for home consumption on credit throughout the year, at a moderate rate of interest, and to maintain a small buffer stock for the following year, in case the harvest of the current year should fail.

Through the buffalo banks, group members aim at becoming the owner of a buffalo they would otherwise have to rent. Buffalos also produce manure which reduces, but does not fully eliminate, the need for chemical fertilizer.

In both villages the small farmers, by forming groups, have strengthened their claim-making capacity and obtained access to subsidized fertilizer, although lately farmers have started questioning the profitability of the use of chemical fertilizer. The objective of the Credit Union in Ban Isan village and of the savings funds set up by the groups in Ban Nua village is to provide a credit facility to their membership. This is an activity which is complementary to the rice bank since rice can easily be converted into money and vice versa. In Ban Nua the savings funds also serve as starting capital for collective investments and the constitution of working capital.

Structure

The small self-help groups of 10 to 15 members in Ban Nua are kinship groups and homogeneous in terms of material welfare and occupation. The landless have their own groups, as have the small farmers. In Ban Isan the situation is somewhat more complex. There is a considerable overlap in membership between credit union, rice bank, buffalo bank and fertilizer bank membership. They have respectively 50, 30, 29 and 16 members. Each activity-group has its own Committee of 4 persons (president, vice-president, treasurer, secretary). Positions on the board in the four groups rotate among the same ten leaders. The villagers of Ban Isan who participate in self-help activities can thus be seen as a single group of approximately 70 persons composed of 4 main sub-groups with overlapping membership.

The uncertain legal status of the Thai SH groups, just as in the Brazilian and Indonesian case studies, is causing some concern. 'The self-help organization was always accused by the government of being 'illegal' which affected the morale and operations of the organization. Thus, in the general assembly last October, villagers proposed the registration of their organization as a legal entity using the savings and credit society (Credit Union) as the foundation' (Thai report, p.36). The expectation is that once the activities are carried out by a legal body, such as a Credit Union, it will be easier to carry on commercial operations, and if need be, to enter into contract agreements with third parties, governmental or non-governmental, for the collective purchase of fertilizer, sale of surplus rice, etc. Against this, one could argue that official registration may indeed please the government and facilitate certain operations with them, but at the same time it will open the door to increased government interference in the internal affairs of the Ban Isan SHOs.

The SH groups in Ban Nua village have a comparative advantage by reason of their smallness. It makes them less vulnerable to government intervention, and to pressure from the same when the latter seeks to extend its territory and controlling powers by insisting that informal SH groups should become legal entities. The DISACs see it as their task to feed the discussion on the pros and cons of official registration, but leave the ultimate decision to the villagers themselves.

Activities

Some of the salient aspects of the activites of SHOs in the two villages are given below:

In Ban Isan, the credit union charges 15% interest, the rice bank 30%. The difference is much less than it would appear, because when rice is bought it has a much higher moisture content than when it is distributed three months to one year later.

The Ban Nua rice bank even charges 50% interest. This is done in order to build up group capital. The rate is still half of what villagers used to pay to the private rice lenders before SH groups in the village started their operations.

The average size of loans to members from the credit union in Ban Isan is Baht 1,000 (US$ 38), the upper limit being twice as much. The maximum loan members can get from the rice bank is 1,200 kg (counter value approx. US$ 85). No interest is paid on monetary savings, nor on savings in kind (rice). The SHO member who receives a buffalo in Ban Nua repays to DISAC approximately the same amount he would otherwise have had to pay for renting one. The difference is that now, after four to five years, the farmer will be the buffalo's owner and will have stopped paying rent. The arrangement can be considered as some sort of hire purchase agreement which ties in with the customary practice of buffalo hiring.

The Thai action-researchers, however, emphasized that buffalos are still primarily viewed as group property. Calves (which normally come every second year) belong to the group, not to the individual, and when a buffalo dies, the whole group bears the burden. In that way the risks are spread over group members. In Ban Isan village a problem arose when borrowers started to use the rice bank facilities for on-lending at a higher rate to non-members. The same has happened in other DISAC-supported villages. This behaviour was considered by the villagers to go against the philosophy and objective of the rice bank and must be restrained. With the interdiction of on-lending, the rice bank was no longer attractive to those farmers who did not really need the rice-borrowing facility to cater for their own consumption needs. As a result the big 'surplus farmers' (cultivating 100 rai or more) who have sufficient storage capacity of their own, no longer participate in the rice bank.

In Ban Nua, all the small groups save, in rice or in money. Even the landless do so by contributing Baht 5 per month (US$ 0.19) to the group fund. The members of the women-only group also save to build up working capital for the collective purchase of pig feed.

Organizational performance

Financial, administrative and managerial autonomy
The Ban Isan rice bank has repaid the Baht 40,000 (US$ 1,536) it borrowed from DISAC Ubon for working capital. Moreover it has built up a revolving fund of Baht 90,000 (US$ 3,460!), two-thirds of which is used for the rice business and one-third for cash loans to members (this also demonstrates how the division of functions between Credit Union and rice bank operations has got blurred). The group has thus become financially self-reliant.

In Ban Nua, the most successful SHO in terms of capital accumulation is the oldest group, no.1. Initial losses which occurred due to poor technical management, have been more than compensated in later years by regular surpluses. Through regular savings the group has accumulated a reserve fund to the amount of Baht 20,000 (US$ 769). The other groups, although at a slower pace, are evolving in the same direction.

In both villages the SHOs have achieved a high level of administrative and managerial autonomy. DISAC assistance is still required for discussing strategies vis-à-vis government authorities and for training. Even those groups in Ban Nua who started by themselves without any DISAC support acknowledge the need for such assistance.

The fertilizer programme which services many villages of the DISAC Ubon, is predominantly managed and controlled by the SHPI's staff (DISAC Ubon). The gross profit of approximately 15% on the fertilizer business is used at DISAC level to feed a 'revolving fund'. DISAC staff also play a crucial role in the acquisition of fertilizer from the parastatal distributing agency MOF (Marketing Organization For Farmers). It is the only DISAC-supported economic activity with a rather weak self-help component.

Participation

The smaller groups in Ban Nua meet more frequently (twice a month) than the larger groups in Ban Isan. Apart from the women-only group in Ban Nua, all other groups in the two villages are exclusively male or strongly male-dominated. In Ban Nua, where groups are smaller, participation by women in discussion is more frequent. As in the Brazilian and Indonesian cases, leaders make the decisions.

Development performance

Socio-economic impact

In the absence of more detailed household surveys, the economic impact of the self-help group activities can only be expressed in the terms used by the villagers themselves, such as: 'The members of the rice bank now have rice to eat throughout the whole year'. A remarkable achievement indeed, if one knows that in the past most families were short of rice during the pre-harvest period. One would have liked to have such a statement substantiated by more precise quantitative data on the situation before and after the start of the rice bank. The villagers themselves, however, feel no need for such hard evidence. To them their experience is sufficient as scientific proof. Another highly valued effect of the rice bank is that middlemen who come from outside to buy surplus rice from the village are now forced to use the weighing scales which belong to the group. Further, the interest rate for rice on credit has dropped remarkably in both villages, from 50% charged by private middlemen to 30% in Ban Isan (on a yearly basis) and from 100% to 50% in the Ban Nua case. But perhaps even more important is that a larger part of the harvest is now being stored in the village (at the rice bank) for future consumption, while in the past, as members of the Ban Isan groups observed, more rice left the village for repayment of debts. In Ban Isan village the buffalo bank and the fertilizer programme, and the subsequent increase in agricultural production, have also helped to heighten the level of economic self-reliance of the village as a whole.

102

In spite of the very obvious advantages to be gained from the various activities, no satisfactory explanation could be given by the villagers as to why the greater part of the population of Ban Isan village so far had not joined the rice bank or any of the other SHO activities, nor set up their own groups. The reason given was: 'They lack the confidence'.

In Ban Nua village participation in SH groups is more widespread. The number of groups has rapidly expanded over the past three years and two-thirds of the village households are now actively engaged in one or more self-help activities. For the poorer households, particularly for the landless wage labourers, the rice bank is said to offer an important additional benefit: 'Members now need less time to search for sources of credit'.

The better-off farmers in Ban Nua, who in fact started the SH movement, also feel more comfortable now that the poorer community members have their own rice bank, since it frees them from the obligation to lend rice to the poor which may in fact not be returned. An expression of social concern is the fact that members of SHOs who have borrowed rice or money because of sickness occurring in the family, are exempted from interest payments. A similar arrangement exists in some Indonesian UBs.

Political impact

The activities of the self-help groups in the Thai villages, as was also found in the villages in the other two countries, do not seem to have caused any significant change of power relations *within* the village. At the micro-regional level, however, the situation is different. Through their SHOs, villagers have been able to strengthen their claim-making and bargaining position vis-à-vis government authorities and private merchants. An example of the first is the non-acceptance by the villagers of the 'blue-print' model of organization for rice bank administration and management promoted by the government, while private merchants are confronted by a much more organized village and can no longer impose their conditions one-sidedly.

Cultural impact

In both villages the self-help activities have given rise to change and have reinforced the villagers' self-confidence. The objectives of the groups are, as repeatedly observed by leaders and members, 'not commercial and not for profit, but the organization is helping us to live. We aim further... we will build an organization for our children' (Thai report, p. 62).

Reflecting on the many failures in other DISAC supported villages, the Thai action-researchers stressed the importance of the moral dimension in self-help organization and promotion. The DISAC staff have realized that the economic motive in itself is insufficient to produce lasting self-help organizations. In their view also, the well known essential ingredients for lasting success of a self-help organization, namely group discipline, unity, solidarity, and a dedicated leadership, need religious grounding. Self-help activities should boost the people's morale and capacity for positive creative thinking, both of which tend to be undermined by the complex of external economic and political factors, leading to corruption, negligence of duties, bossy behaviour, drinking, and the 'big fish eats the smaller ones' mentality, etc. The Thai report argues that wherever the activities of the two DISACs appear to have lasting success, their intervention has been combined with the increased valuation and appreciation of religious teaching.

103

DISAC staff both at Chiengmai and Ubon have arrived at the same conclusion, namely that 'we have to play down the economic dimension and stress other dimensions' (Thai report, p. 89). Self-help promotion, they conclude, that does not take into account the binding and motivating force of Buddhism (or Christianity) is one-sided and likely to be ineffective.

In a later section (Chapter 9) we shall further discuss the 'holistic approach' to development which is rapidly gaining ground in Thai NGO circles. The holistic philosphy has a considerable bearing on the type and nature of the ecomonic activities which are promoted – or deliberately *not* promoted – and on the organization of NGO field work.

Brazil – small farmer leaders discuss study findings with MOC action-researchers.

Thailand – the holistic approach. There is no development without spiritual development.

Indonesia – a UB economic activity. The forefront shows the *krupuk* before it is cooked. The boxes behind serve to carry the *krupuk* to the local market.

8   How to promote and support self-help: the eight instruments reviewed

In Chapter 3, we defined and discussed eight instruments of self-help promotion. We shall now review how and to what extent these instruments were used by the SHPIs in interaction with the SHOs and their leadership, and we shall consider their factual contribution towards reaching the system's objective, viz. 'the building up of an associative economy which supports the socio-economic emancipation of the rural poor'. Each section will conclude with a series of possible and recommendable changes in self-help promotion policies and practices for the SHPIs concerned.

Instrument 1: Identification of target population and self-help groups

The principal 'raison d'être' of local NGOs is their assumed proximity in spirit and action to the target population, while government or government-controlled development agencies, as well as their programmes and projects, are further removed from the specific interests and aspirations of the poor. In SH promotion the danger of by-passing the poor, however, is always present, irrespective of the juridical status of the promotion agency, and this risk tends to be greater the more the activities centre around economic issues. We are faced here with the practical problem that 'organization is more problematical among those who need organization most – the landless, tenants at will, marginal smallholders... and especially the women in these groups' (Esman and Uphoff, pp. 35-36). The cases discussed in the foregoing are illustrative of the fact that target population involvement should not be taken for granted and that 'economic projects' in particular move away easily from the category of people they are meant to serve. In the Indonesian case it became clear that it was simply not enough to wait for groups to ask Bina Swadaya for assistance, and to rely on 'mouth-to-mouth' publicity for the UB type of organization to spread among the rural poor. NGOs in general, as one MOC researcher observed, still fail to take into account that the 'rural poor' are not a homogeneous group and that sub-categories among them have different interests or priorities. The MOC action-researchers came to the conclusion that the ongoing 'Luta Popular', which they supported in their region, took this aspect insufficiently into account, and that more attention should be given to the specific problems of rural women and rural youth, as well as to the landless families who are under-represented among APAEB membership. A SHPI has a specific duty to raise the level of awareness of self-help leadership and their members to the possible existence within their communities of persons in greater need than themselves, people who under present conditions might not benefit in sufficient measure from ongoing self-help activities (MOC 1985).

This policy of raising the leadership's awareness of the contradictions which might exist within their own communities, was practised by staff of the DISAC Chiengmai when in 1982 they started to work and grant assistance to the SHOs in Ban Nua village. Shortly afterwards, it resulted in the creation of rice banks for the landless.

Target population identification is 'extremely important for the design of specific programmes for the rural poor' (ILO, 1984, p. 111) and can be greatly facilitated by the use of appropriate indicators. Indicators are highly contextual and there are no fixed rules on how to develop them. In the Brazilian research area action-researchers identified as an important easy-to-identify indicator the possession by the household of an animal for human or non-human cargo. The poorest have no such animal, the poor have only a donkey, the not-so-poor have a donkey and a mule and relatively well-to-do households have a horse (Brazilian report, p. 95). In the Indonesian research villages, housing in combination with the frequency with which the family ate rice was found a useful indicator of prosperity. (Rice consumption is considered a luxury; the basic staple for the poor in some areas is cassava). Landlessness and/or landholding criteria are another category often applied for identification of the target population and they seem to be of relevance in the situation of all four participant SHPIs.

In none of the cases studied were indicators systematically used by SHPI field workers for purposes of identification, for checking target population participation, or for monitoring changes over time in levels of prosperity. Some important steps in this direction have been made under the present study.

The absence of a well-developed instrumentarium for target population identification does not imply that there is no target-group orientation. According to MOC/APAEB experience, rural households can be divided into five strata. It was decided to concentrate on the middle and second lowest level, viz. family farms with an upper limit of 10 hectares approximately. MOC/APAEB are still searching for ways to increase their serviceability towards the poorest, e.g. the landless and near-landless.

The Indonesian and Thai studies have also shown how important it is to identify the already existing organizations in the village and the role they play, prior to any definite decision on whether or not to grant support to any of these groups or encourage the creation of new ones. Existing organizations are not necessarily 'traditional'. The social structures of the villages undergo constant change. New groups are created, some with, others without outside support; some become stronger, others disappear quietly. New challenges result in new groups being created (see the history of Baleharjo in Indonesia and of Ban Nua in Thailand). But where such initiatives are spontaneously taken 'by the people', the poorest sections seem to be the last to organize themselves.

107

In the Thai view, it is an error to work exclusively with self-help groups, unless this is conceived as a temporary strategy with the final aim of involving the entire village community. An exclusive focus on groups is likely to lead to a situation where 'a majority of the members are mainly middle-class with only about five per cent being poor' (Thai report, p. 42). In the DISAC approach we can thus distinguish two stages in the identification process:

– An existing group, or a group in formation, identifies DISAC as a valuable SHPI or vice versa. It is a two-way process of mutual identification. The two parties, SHO and SHPI, then get to know each other better and may or may not come to a consensus. If the SHO is only profit-oriented, the DISAC will not accept it as a partner.

– During the second stage of the identification process the first SHO in the village acts as a self-help 'core group'. In conjunction with the SHPI the poorer sections in the village are identified, which then become the joint target for self-help promotion.

The consequences of the above for the organization of the work of the SHPIs in the three countries can be summarized as follows:

– Whenever a new SHO presents itself to the SHPI, seeking the latter's assistance, there is a need to assess carefully to which category the leaders of the SHO (in formation) and the greater part of their followers belong. So far, this has not, or not always been done with sufficient care.

– Whenever SHO membership is found to belong to the somewhat better-off sections of rural society, which is often the case, they should only be accepted as 'target groups' to the extent that they can evolve into 'core groups' and into a catalyst for mobilizing the self-help capacities of the poor majority (whether the poor should have their own groups or not is a different matter).

– Concerning the existing groups with which the SHPI is already working, especially in the Bina Swadaya situation, some sort of re-identification and assessment seem necessary with a view to determining which SHOs do and which do not contribute to the socio-economic emancipation of the rural poor, in other words, which SHOs help or do not help to achieve the declared objectives of the SHPI.

– The instrumentarium for target group identification needs further development in all the cases studied, not only for identification purposes, but also for monitoring the development performance of the SH promotion system.

Instrument 2: Participatory research and planning

Participatory 'research' – the active participation of the target population in diagnostic and problem-solving thinking – is often advocated but seldom done. When SHPIs and SHOs enter into contact, it is normally to initiate an activity, a 'project', not to conduct what the Thai workshop participants recommend and call a 'social analysis'. They deliberately avoid the word 'research': 'Formerly, we used the term 'research', which was seen as the work of the academics... From this we found that there is a domination which inhibits self-help of the people' (Chattip, Thai workshop report, p. 8). When saying 'we', Chattip refers to the practice of a number of small, innovative NGOs in Thailand, which stress that the 'preparation of the people's idea' should precede 'the project'. The analysis should be undertaken together with the 'village intellectuals' and might take as long as six months (according to the experience of another NGO, the North-East Community Development Workers Group). To do it properly is time-consuming, but six months is still a short period, if one realizes that it embodies a process of people starting to think differently on the subject of how to restructure the village economy. Subsequently, when the implementation process begins, 'economic activities may not cover from the outset all members of the community but consciousness raising should' (Chattip, Thai workshop).

The Brazilian and Indonesian case studies showed how crucial it is to assess the feasibility of an economic activity in its various dimensions: economic, social, political, technical, and operational (this did not appear so clearly from the Thai cases, because they were success cases, but the overall performance of SHOs promoted by the two DISACs is not necessarily better than that of the SHOs in the two other countries).

The start of the rice huller by a UB group in Indonesia was indeed preceded by an assessment of economic feasibility. But the social aspect was not looked into. The common bond was weak. Membership proved to be too heterogeneous for successful collective economic action. The rice huller mainly served the interests of one of the group leaders. The same seems to have happened with the krupuk factory set up in the second research village.

Other economic activities of the UBs (bean and livestock production) were found to be under-studied from an economic point of view. Especially when labour input is taken into consideration, their profitability from the members' point of view was even more doubtful. From the household studies we learned that members of low-income households are over-occupied; in other words that the opportunity cost of their labour input is relatively high, higher than for the more well-to-do sections of the population, who have time to spare.

In the case of APAEB, Brazil, the high expectations of economic benefits which the consumer shops were believed to produce for their membership, were based on two wrong assumptions: that intermediaries in the retail trade were making huge profits by overcharging and that rampant inflation could be effectively countered when people had their own shops.

The first assumption of excessively high profit margins being realized in the private retail sector proved incorrect as far as the private shops in the smaller district towns were concerned. Profit margins of those in the villages were very high indeed. The second assumption was based on the misconception that a macro-problem, inflation, could be solved by a micro-solution, a consumer shop. To realize a certain volume of sale, APAEB operations in the consumer sector from the very beginning had to be organized on a regional scale, which could have no other effect than to weaken the participatory and self-help aspects of the activities from the start of operations.

We also saw that a medium-size 'Casa de Farinha' (cassava mill) could give important benefits to SHO membership, but another mill of three times that capacity (Tanque Velho) caused operational problems whose solution would require an even larger investment (lorries, rasping machines), making the organization unwieldy for self-administration.

The Brazilian action-researchers observed a tendency among APAEB leaders to over-estimate the absorption capacity of their own groups. Especially when leaders felt that finances could be easily obtained, groups tended to engage in new economic ventures at a rate which exceeded their capacity for self-administration and self-management. The results were the overburdening of leaders, poor internal control, and neglect of educational tasks (Brazilian report, p.124). Even inter-group contacts may suffer from lack of time. In self-help promotion, the greatest challenge remains to identify economic activities which are beneficial to the poor majority. For this, one cannot exclusively rely on the leaders' appreciation of the situation. The identification of such activities calls for prolonged stays in the village by the SHPI staff to familiarize themselves with the living and working conditions of the rural poor. Household surveys administered to a small sample of poor households and conducted in a dialogue atmosphere, can be considered as helpful for deepening insight. For example, household surveys conducted in Indonesia under the present study brought to light the possibility of and the need for re-structuring the cattle breeding and raising systems. Tenant cattle raisers, who receive only half of the added value, possess all the skills and contacts necessary to carry on such an activity on their own. The only factor of production they lack in sufficient measure is capital for investment. For a Brazilian small farmer family, it might be even more important to become independent from the 'sementes de meia' system (half of the harvest goes to the supplier of seed) than to have access to consumer goods at a somewhat lower price in town (where most APAEB shops are situated).

These examples are given to illustrate that better knowledge of the economy of the poor is a prerequisite for effective SHPI intervention. SHPI involvement, directly or indirectly, in 'project' implementation does not provide such insight in sufficient measure. MOC in its development plan for 1986, taking into account the findings of the present study, states that a SHPI should avoid the 'atropelamento de atividades' (a cumulation of activities 'falling one on top of the other'), and stresses the need for more 'reflexâo preparatoria' (literally: preparatory reflection). The above considerations suggest the following orientations for participatory research and planning:
– SHPI field staff should develop the skills for, and be stimulated to undertake, socio-economic analyses which should be conducted in at least some of the 'core' villages where SHOs are in operation, or expected to get started with SHPI support (in French: 'étude de milieu');
– For SHO leadership to decide in a responsible manner on what economic activities to undertake or not to undertake, they will need greater advance knowledge of costs and benefits and possible risks. In their appreciation of the situation they will need more assistance from SHPI staff in the assessment of feasibility in its various dimensions, in other words, not only in relation to the economic aspects but also in relation to the social, political, technical and operational aspects of the undertaking;
– The process of participatory research (or 'analysis') and planning should in the first place seek to identify activities which can be implemented by the SHOs themselves, without much need for continued managerial or financial support. Regional level projects, however much desired by local leaders, as in the case of APAEB, do not seem to be very appropriate as a starter-activity for self-help promotion;
– SHPI staff in general, as appeared from the study and ensuing workshop discussions, appear to be ill-equiped to assist SHO leadership and members in the analysis of their economic environment, the specific problems of the rural poor, and planning of economic activities. SHPI staff are not particularly geared towards performing such functions, nor have they been adequately trained for them. Follow-up programmes should provide for on-the-job training in these matters.

Instrument 3: Education and mutual training

Education and training practice, as organized by most development agencies, is still paternalistic and curative in nature. Logically, when project preparation is done in a directive and top-down manner, the supporting educational and training programme will share the same features. From the point of view of self-help promotion, one-way 'class-room' methods of teaching are anti-developmental. They do not encourage creative thinking, they aim at 'adoption'. Information programmes diffused by the mass media and advertizing campaigns are also inspired by a similar sort of philosphy. They bear witness to 'a flagrant disregard of people's knowledge and experience' (Brazilian report, p. 182) and to a veneration of modern, technical, specialized knowledge. MOC/APAEB are proud that they have been able to contribute to the development of a storage technique for seeds and staple food, free from the use of chemicals and receiving its main direction from traditional practice.

The Thai action-researchers for these reasons raised objections to the term 'education and training'. When indeed the aim is to create a learning situation in which knowledge is transmitted in a two-way direction between process facilitators (the former teacher) and development actors (SHO leaders and members), 'knowledge sharing and generation' would be a more appropriate term. Not surprisingly, the two DISACs in Thailand who came to this conclusion, had to reconsider their earlier formal training programmes. Preference and priority are, and will be given in future, to village level informal meetings which are largely self-organized and self-financed by the villages. Part of the same strategy is the organization of inter-village exposures (Thai report, p. 71).

DISAC Chiengmai has also initiated meetings at regional level of 'project holders'. On such occasions, representatives of SHOs which carry on one or more economic activities meet with leaders from other groups who have submitted a project proposal to the DISAC office. Such a meeting exemplifies the interrelation between the 'education and training' instrument and the earlier discussed 'participatory planning' instrument. For the financing of such a meeting the DISAC bears part of the board and lodging costs, while costs of transportation are met entirely by the SHOs themselves.

This is consistent with the basic principle of 'contributing from own resources' in respect of each and every promotional activity. In line with the 'holistic approach' the Thai report also emphasized the importance of spiritual education as an integral part of the educational process (Thai report, p. 94), and of education as a tool to develop and maintain a high standard of morality in the process of economic exchanges. It is interesting to note that in relation to spiritual training, the term 'education and training' seems to have lost some of its negative connotations and that 'teaching' in the traditional way (by the monk) seems an acceptable practice. The DISAC of Chiengmai has another target group for training which does not appear to exist in other cases, known as 'organic intellectuals', i.e. young people who are prepared to stay in the village and, with the help of the DISAC, are offered opportunities for more advanced professional training outside the village for a period of time. They are continuously guided by the DISAC in their reflection on the meaning and significance of their newly acquired knowledge and skills for the organization of village life and their own position within this.

Both the Bina Swadaya and MOC reports express dissatisfaction with the ongoing systems of education and training. Present systems are too much focussed on leaders, so-called 'multiplicators', who seldom or never multiply. The training programme of Bina Swadaya in the Yogyakarta research area gets its direction chiefly from target setting (number of courses, number of participants) and from what the teachers (the field-workers) have to offer rather than what participants regard as priority matters. In principle, the choice is with the leaders, but the range of options is very limited due to the limitations of the field-workers. Course participants 'see the positive impact of training courses primarily as the chance to meet people from other groups, to exchange ideas with them' (Indonesian report, p. 101). But course contents are not linked to planned or ongoing economic activities and the courses have no follow-up (idem, p. 102). Bina Swadaya has now initiated a new policy of widening the opportunities for subject matter training by inviting resource persons from other 'supporting organizations' and neighbouring UB groups.

The APAEB/MOC gatherings in Brazil are of a different nature. Leaders exchange ideas, experiences, and discuss problems on a wide variety of matters related to economic activities, politics, health, etc.. They present to each other songs and poems of their own composition. However, the information, experience and inspiration gathered by leaders from this kind of interaction is transferred to membership to a very limited extent only. In fact, what has occurred over the past years is an enlargement of the knowledge and information gap between leadership and membership, which is in contradiction with MOC's objective of creating a more 'egalitarian' society. MOC is now looking for ways and means to strengthen the responsibility of leaders for the effective transmission to membership of the knowledge and skills they have acquired during special leadership courses (Brazilian report, p. 128) (a principle often applied by many NGOs to ensure such transmission is to have members contribute to the training costs of their leaders/representatives).

In development education, the 'father knows best' tradition has had its day. At the same time, one should also recognize that the imparting of a specific skill may sometimes call for a more directive approach: examples are cost calculation, bookkeeping, maintenance of machines etc.. The choice is therefore not so much between the one or the other approach. Rather it is the task of the SHPI to work out, with the leaders and members of SHOs, a well-balanced package of education and training facilities which contains elements of both.
The consequences for the SHPIs in the field of education and training practice seem to be the following:
- In order to prevent a growing knowledge and information gap between leaders and followers, decentralized, extramural village level education and training should be given greater emphasis in the programmes of the SHPIs. This will lessen – but not completely eliminate – the need for centrally organized training courses in 'training centres'.
- The SHPIs in all three countries may consider developing a programme of 'functional education' which is directed specifically at the ordinary members of SHOs. The functional aspect refers to the direct link between course contents and the economic activities which the SHO has planned for, or has started. Ideally, such a programme should include literacy for the illiterate part of SHO membership as well as numeracy training as a means for all members to get a better understanding of the economics of self-help activities.

- As to APAEB, Brazil, in order to reach financial autonomy, there is an obvious need for its executive staff, especially branch managers, to be trained in such fields as cost calculation, pricing of goods, stock and cash controls, shop management, etc., and for its Executive Committee to learn about fundamental business concepts (overhead costs, depreciation, break-even point, working and reserve capital).

Instrument 4: Resource mobilization and resource provision

As one DISAC director put it: 'If the poor manage to survive, then this is because they have something; and if they have something, they can save'. The primary function of a SHO is to provide the organizational framework for the pooling of members' savings, which will then enable them to obtain credit, if need be.*

Savings
Contributions from members' own resources can take various forms: financial (money), material (e.g. rice for the rice banks) or human (labour, know-how). The capital for the first rice banks at Ban Nua, as we have seen, was not obtained through outside support but from member contributions, while savings by members of the poorer landless groups were complemented by contributions from the richer village groups.
The Indonesian UBs have operated for many years on their own funds and continue in part to do so.
APAEB members have contributed labour and material for the construction of the buildings which house the consumer, storage and processing units. As yet, no monetary savings scheme has been started by APAEB; the resources are there, but so far have not been tapped. The successful introduction of savings schemes by the 'Caixa Economica' (State-owned bank) and several private banks points to the existence of a savings potential in rural areas. Part of the APAEB membership participate in these schemes as holders of a 'Caderneta de Poupança' (= savings deposit books). Factually, such schemes have the macro-effect of draining small farmers' savings into large scale industrial projects. If APAEB leaders and members were to invest some more of their own savings in their own economic activities, they would achieve a higher degree of financial autonomy and probably also demonstrate greater care and caution in making investment decisions. Another indication of a savings potential in rural Brazil is the existence of 'caixas' which are particularly popular among rural women. Caixas are informal thrift and credit associations. A lottery system determines who gets the loan first.
Development literature abounds in examples of astonishing savings capacities in rural areas, also among the poor, who seem to be the first to recognize the importance of saving as a means of reducing the risks of life (ILO, 1984). In the

113

---

* In Working Document no. 1 of the recent Cebemo study '*A comment on the S 24 study of the German Federal Ministry*' by K. Verhagen (1985), the possible negative effects of external financing have already been dealt with. The discussion will not be repeated here (Oegstgeest, The Netherlands: Cebemo, Mimeo).

Indonesian research area, Gunung Kidul district, the 73 Credit Unions supported by Foster Parents' Plan accumulated Rp 100 million of savings capital (US$ 90,000). Their loan portfolio amounted to Rp 107 million (US$ 95,000). These and many more examples show that there is a large self-help potential in the financial sector, and that the availability of outside finance – where it takes the form of 'easy money' – might well be one of the main obstacles to achieving greater financial self-reliance for the rural populace.

Credit

In discussing the role of credit in SH promotion, the first question one should ask is whether there is a need for it. The experiences of DISAC Chiengmai in the research villages and some other localities served by the same DISAC show that SHOs need very little external material support to start up meaningful economic activities. However, in cases where some form of financial support is necessary, one might add a second question: where should such support come from, from a local or a foreign financing (donor) agency? When support originates from a foreign agency, monies are mostly seen to be channelled through the SHPI, acting 'de facto', as a 'sub-donor'. The NGO concerned would probably not like such an epithet, but this is how they are often looked upon by the recipients.

The Indonesian Bina Swadaya has a long tradition of channelling foreign support to local groups. One channel has been the KSK credit programme referred to earlier (p. 68 and p. 92). The programme has undergone many changes in its regulations and procedures since its inception in 1976. With the recent setting up of the 'Centre for Solidarity Capital Formation', UB groups are now encouraged to deposit their savings with this Centre, for which they receive some form of dividend at the end of the year, depending on the Centre's surplus.

Lending rates to UB groups amount to 2.5% per month for credit which is used for on-lending to individual members, 2% when used for working capital for group enterprises (economic activities), and 1.5% when used by groups for investment purpose. The term is usually 10 to 12 months and can be extended when given for investment purposes (up to 3 years). The savings/credit ratio is 1:8 for very poor groups and 1:2 for groups which are almost self-reliant (Indonesian report, pp. 106-107).

The assessment of the UB groups' savings capacity was done by the field-worker. Of the groups investigated in the first research village, Baleharjo, all the UB groups received five times their 'solidarity savings', while the farmers' group in Pacing received credit at a ratio of 1:8. Access to such a credit scheme as KSK may accelerate the undertaking of economic activities, but it also undeniably detracts from the need for the mobilization of resources by own efforts. For example, it is doubtful whether the farmers' group in Pacing would ever have started their collective field if they had had access to KSK credit from the beginning of the group's operations. Moreover, the easy inflow of money from external sources also tends to weaken the internal control mechanisms. The Indonesian study provided some confirmation of the assumption that credit which stems from members' own savings, is normally more equitably distributed than credit which comes from outside. However, the present recording system of Bina Swadaya is still insufficiently developed to monitor such important facts whenever they occur.

Just as in the case of Bina Swadaya, the funds of the DISACs in Thailand which serve to finance the economic activities of SHOs, come primarily from foreign donor NGOs. This is also true for MOC (Brazil), but MOC does more than the others to assist SHOs in getting access to the local credit system and subsidy programmes, such as those administered by Polonordeste and the Prefeituras (district administration), etc. It has made the promotional system somewhat less dependent on foreign financial assistance. At the same time project appraisal and approval have been partly localized and have become the prime responsibility of local financing agencies. With such a structure, foreign agency financing can be restricted to institutional support for the local SHPI, i.e. MOC.

In discussing external resource provision there should be no hesitation about raising two more fundamental questions. The first one is whether self-help promotion is at all compatible with the 'sub-donor' function as at present performed by most SHPIs in developing countries. The Thai report says that under present conditions field-workers still spend a lot of energy in explaining that the DISAC, although its limited financing role, is no a banker; that money which comes from a church-affiliated organization ('from the priest') also has to be repaid; and, additionally, that accepting financial assistance from a DISAC carries no obligation whatsoever to convert to Christianity. (p. 38).

The second question relates to the role of local financing agencies.* The proposition of greater involvement of local agencies, banks or otherwise in financing economic activities, may not be considered very practical in situations where the existing financial agencies are inimical to genuine forms of self-help promotion. But is not such a situation often taken for granted too easily? In the cases studied, the public sector in general was not found to serve the poor in a meaningful way, except where the SHPI had set itself the task, formally or informally, of acting as an intermediary in the process of linkage building (MOC, DISAC Ubon, Bina Swadaya for some groups) or to monitor that process through a watchdog function (both DISACs in Thailand). However, the possible negative consequences of such a policy should also be realized. The danger of loss of autonomy when accepting government funding will be further reviewed below in 'linkage building' (Chapter 8). If the source of funding is bank credit, SHOs and their members not only may have to sacrifice part of their autonomy of action but may also end up in a situation of bondage to a financing system over which they have no control. In self-help promotion, one must exercise great caution in facilitating external credit, especially when funding originates from institutional lenders which have been given the mandate 'to reach the small farmer' or other rural poor. Thai action-researchers in their report observed that there is a form of external resource provision 'which is exploitative, which leads to domination and which is not liberating'. 'Exploitative credit' in their experience may also come from institutional lenders such as development banks. For that reason, another Thai NGO (CULT) has felt it necessary to initiate a debt-redemption programme to liberate the small farmer not from the money-lenders, but from the national agricultural development bank (BAAC)! The Thai farmer who says, 'since I have had that tractor, I have become a slave of the

---

* One of the recommendations of the Nanjing TCDC workshop on strengthening institutional credit services to low-income groups (UN-ESCAP 1986) reads: 'Financial transactions of self-help groups may be handled by self-help support institutions *until* financial institutions are prepared to accommodate these' (author's italics).

bank' testifies to a situation which is not unique for Thailand. Recognizing this fact is not to deny the more positive role banks or agencies with similar functions have played and continue to play in the history of rural development, especially where banks are co-operatively owned.

In the financing of economic activities of SHOs and their membership one can broadly distinguish three different approaches in shaping institutional interaction:
– One is the continuing dependence of SHOs on funds administered by a SHPI/ local NGO, which acts as an intermediary between a foreign financing agency and a local SHO.
– The second is that of the existing local institutional financial system (banks, special financing agencies) being encouraged to adjust their policies to become more responsive to the needs of SHOs and even allow for some form of equity participation by SHOs in the capital of the financing agency.*
– The third is where SHOs are encouraged to develop their own financial system at inter-group level, which will allow them to set their own rules and regulations and remain in full control of choice of activities and use of resources.
There are also all sorts of combinations and variations of the above. Bina Swadaya has opted for the first approach, but at the same time is encouraging savings at group level and at inter-group level through its KSK scheme. MOC/ APAEB so far has no clear strategy in this respect, but it comes near to the second option, when it provides backstopping to APAEB and its SH groups in getting their legitimate share of cheap public financing. The two DISACs in Thailand are moving towards the third possibility: they promote savings at grassroots level and apply a revolving system whereby loan reimbursements by one group are used to finance the activities of other groups. By making the financing system completely open, the DISACs try to strengthen the sense of responsibility of the older groups, which through timely repayment facilitate the financing of new groups. This can be considered an important step towards setting up a common investment fund, which will eventually be administered and managed by the SHO representatives themselves.

Concerning resource mobilization and provision, the following follow-up activities might be considered for the near future:
– the undertaking by MOC of a participatory study to assess the desirability and feasibility of a savings programme which would enhance the self-financing capacity of APAEB and its affiliated groups;
– a re-consideration of the SHPIs' role as lending institutions, with the explicit recognition of the fact that self-help promotion and financing are two functions which are difficult to reconcile, especially at field level;
– a review of the financing mechanism, giving special attention to one, or a combination of the two following options: (a) the transfer of the banking function, in part or in whole, to specialized local financing organizations, which can also act as recipients of foreign funding for projects; (b) the formation of a revolving fund which is partly fed by SHO contributions and administered by SHO representatives, leaving them the prime responsibility for project approval and fund management.**

116

* A development along such lines was the major thrust of the recommendations of the earlier mentioned Nanjing UN-ESCAP Workshop (1986).
**Actually, one Cebemo-supported NGO in Thailand, not involved in the present study, is already practising this concept.

Instrument 5: Management consultancy

This study is not quite alone in finding that efficient management is central to SHO performance. 'Management consultancy' refers to the assistance given by the SHPI in relation to the ongoing economic activities of self-help organizations. However well prepared a 'project' may be, there is a need for such assistance, a need which tends to decrease in time in relation to a particular activity, but to increase in relation to a particular SHO. This paradoxical finding can be explained by the fact that a dynamic SHO, which has got a first activity started with a certain amount of success, will soon wish to embark upon a second activity, and so on. An effective SHO tends to develop from a single-activity to a multi-activity SHO. This type of evolution makes the SHPI-SHO relationship resemble an 'esperial infinita' (Brazilian report, p. 65), an unending spiral. Yet there might be an end because, as we have discussed earlier, there is a limit to what a single SHO can undertake, given the limitations of its leadership. With the evolution of the SHO, the nature of the required advice and assistance will also change.

As stated in the MOC report, the relationship of dependence of the Subaé vanguard group on MOC is not the same as it was four years ago. The changes which have occurred are a reflection of those which have taken place in the overall MOC-APAEB relationship. They have not followed, as is often assumed in development projects, a simple linear pattern – the promoting agency gradually withdrawing its assistance – but rather oscillated, with the two getting nearer to, or further from each other at different points in time. This type of movement can be explained by the somewhat ambiguous position taken up by the APAEB leadership. In the early eighties MOC was accused of manipulation but later, when MOC staff had purposely adopted a lower profile, they were reproached for having 'put the hot apple in their (the leaders') mouth but MOC did not want to do anything about it'. The relationship between MOC and APAEB groups has matured over time. APAEB leaders insist on getting advice but refuse to be commanded (Brazilian report, pp. 72-75).

During the research workshop in Brazil, a local leader emphasized the need for MOC's assistance in such fields as management of finances and formulation of rules of operation for the SHOs affiliated to APAEB (in cooperative law such formalized rules are called 'by-laws'). The study itself also showed that a much more elaborate bookkeeping system is required to enable earlier detection of shortcomings in management, and facilitate the assessment of the profitability of each economic activity undertaken. The present bookkeeping and accountancy system of APAEB disregards depreciation of donor-financed assets as well as management and interest subsidies, which are essential for APAEB to continue its operations. A new system needs to be conceived which, on the contrary, would make such matters manifest, since there can be no real self-reliance without financial self-reliance.

The management assistance at present provided by the Bina Swadaya field-workers to UBs is adequate in relation to the savings and loan business (recording of savings, credit applications, distribution of loans, interest payments, distribution of surplus). But no adequate recording system has so far been designed for the specific economic activities in which some of the UBs are engaged. The result is that one can only make a guess at their economic profitability after a tentative reconstruction of the accounts, based on imprecise oral information.

UB leaders interviewed also expressed their wish for Bina Swadaya fieldworkers to play a more important role in the settlement of disputes within the UBs. SHPI workers may indeed see it as their task to mediate between the disputants, but it is certainly not their task to arbitrate. Neither MOC nor Bina Swadaya seem to have a clearly defined policy in this respect.

The Thai action-researchers reported a similar inclination among SHOs, which write to DISAC and ask for assistance in resolving their quarrels. It would be a better policy for conflicts to be solved through mediation by leaders from other villages. This however presupposes the existence of a supra-village network, which will be discussed below. The Thai DISACs have a policy of encouraging SHOs to maintain a simple bookkeeping system. In line with their 'knowledge sharing and generation' approach, they do not insist that SHOs should follow a uniform system but assist the SHOs in the design of a system that suits their particular situation.

From the case studies we may conclude that all SHOs, irrespective of their state of development and size of operation, are in need of consultancy in relation to financial and organizational matters, as well as, occasionally, the settlement of internal disputes. From the Brazilian and Indonesian case studies it became apparent that at present the two SHPIs are not able to provide consultancy on the organizational and financial management of economic activities to the extent required by SHOs. In the Thai situation, the simplicity of the operations of the SHOs has meant that, so far, they have less need for this type of consultancy service.

The problem is not just a technical one, in the sense of SHPI staff merely lacking the basic 'nuts and bolts' skills for effectively assisting SHOs in managing their economic activities. It is also a mental attitude. The average SHPI staff member is not 'business-minded'. In the Brazilian context, the provision of moral and educational back-up for a political struggle is a more stimulating type of activity than the design of an accounting system for the analysis of a profit and loss account.

The idea that budgeting and cost accounting are as essential for SHO performance as the moral, ethical and social aspects of their work is gradually gaining ground, but its wholehearted acceptance will take some time. The suggested lines for future action are as follows:

– to make the introduction of appropriate bookkeeping and accountancy systems an item of first priority on the list of 'projects' where such systems do not already exist, or do not provide sufficient insight into the financial situation of SHOs which conduct economic activities, viz. in the case of APAEB, Brazil and some of the Indonesian UBs;*

– to consider, in consultation with SHO leaders, how the role of the SHPI in resolving disputes within the SHO or between SHOs could be reduced to a minimum, and to assist in the conception of procedures which would lay the responsibility for mediation and arbitration primarily on the collective SHOs themselves.

* Even before the Indonesian study had been completed and as a direct outcome of its findings, Bina Swadaya had begun to introduce an auditing and recording system for economic activities.

Instrument 6: Linkage building with third parties

The conceptual framework set out in figure 3 (Chapter 3), presumes that local NGOs acting as SHPIs have a duty to assist SHOs in building up a network of linkages, not only between SHOs (movement building) but also between SHOs and third parties which are potential supporters of SHO activities. Official recognition of complementarity of functions among development institutions, however, holds no guarantee that linkage building is actively pursued as part of the promotion policy. As one action-researcher put it: 'We pay lip service to the issue of inter-institutional collaboration in official meetings, but we do not actively pursue it'.

Local NGOs, including those which participated in the present action-research, have an understandable and natural tendency to regard the SHOs they support as *their* groups. SHOs whose leadership are still lacking in self-confidence may feed that attitude by shifting their own responsibilities on to SHPI staff and forcing them into a protective 'godfather' role, which is contrary to the self-help philosophy. The latest annual report of MOC/Brazil (1985), testifies to a heightened awareness of this problem over past years. MOC, therefore, has not only supported the creation of APAEB as a regional organization, but has also encouraged APAEB groups to get in touch with parastatal financing organizations such as Polonordeste.

The reason for supporting SHOs in linkage building is twofold.
– First it is a matter of principle. Organizational self-reliance implies that SHOs should feel free to interact with those non-governmental or governmental bodies, or private persons whom they feel can serve their interests. SHOs belong only to themselves.
– Secondly it is a matter of practice. Lack of linkage may feed suspicion and result in obstruction, particularly on the part of government agencies. A positive linkage, on the other hand, may have the additional advantage of giving access to productive resources distributed by such agencies.

The Indonesian action-researchers do not deny the importance of linkages but are not too sure whether there is a need to assist UBs in building them up. 'The strong and well informed leaders of UBs are capable of contacting support organizations and do so quite effectively by themselves (other NGOs, government extension services, etc.). However, since Bina Swadaya has to start concentrating on the poorer sections..., assistance in linkage building might prove necessary'.
At the workshop in Brazil, SHO leaders complained about the large number of development agencies adressing themselves to the rural population (in the research village of Subaé no less than eleven); a situation which creates a lot of confusion in the minds of the people.
On the other hand, leaders argued that now that they were organized, they felt much more confidence in entering the town-based offices of such organizations and putting in their claims.
The policy of the two Thai DISACs, which is endorsed by the action-researchers, reflects an attitude of great caution. The DISACs see it as their duty to act as the SHOs' consultants in the management of their external relations. 'They have to know whether (the third party) will benefit them or exploit them'. The BAAC

(Development bank), as discussed earlier, may push the small farmers into a cycle of indebtedness, and collaboration with government entails the risk of loss of autonomy (Thai report, p. 76). But the Thai action-researchers also recognize that 'villagers cannot avoid getting in contact with government and merchants. They will be contacted by them if they do not seek it' (idem, p. 86).

Not only in Thailand, but elsewhere too, we see persistent attempts by governments to capture local organizations by a combination of political pressure and promises of easy money or other facilities. Such co-optation efforts are not necessarily always prompted by malignant motives. There might be a sincere wish 'to bring more of the rural poor into the development process'.
But, good intentions notwithstanding, it is still the bureaucrats' view of development that prevails and therefore carries the danger of loss of SHO self-determination. The answer to this dilemma lies probably in one of the premises underlying the linkage building process as conceived in the framework of the 'holistic approach' (see Chapter 9). SHOs or their representatives can only negotiate to their advantage with third parties from a position of strength. Such strength does not and cannot rest on material wealth only. Rather it emanates from a combination of spiritual wealth and a high degree of economic self-reliance. By economic self-reliance is meant a state of the village economy whereby villagers are not crucially dependent on outside support for the supply of food and other basic necessities.
Maintenance of SHO autonomy can be pursued in two ways:
– By minimizing interaction with third parties, relying entirely on its own resources. This is the *autocratic* scenario.
– By frequent interaction with a variety of institutions and maintaining a careful balance between a series of dependencies and interdependencies. This is the *diplomatic* scenario.
The latter seems the more realistic one. The ongoing rapprochement between SHOs and government-controlled organizations in all three countries appears to be an irreversible trend for the years to come. More important than how much interaction there is between SHOs and third parties would seem to be the *nature* of such interaction. Assuming that SHPIs have a duty to assist SHOs in the process of linkage building with third parties, suggested lines of action fall in three directions:
– One is to inform SHO leaders and membership more systematically about the facilities third parties have to offer, and to stimulate discussions about the possible benefits and risks of strengthening relationships. To a certain degree this policy is already being practised by MOC and DISAC, not so much by Bina Swadaya.
– The second line of action is to actively further the creation of a climate of greater sympathy for and understanding of the self-help approach within government or paragovernmental administrations. This last aspect is already taken care of by the SHPIs through participation in seminars, consultations, etc., at national or state level, but, unfortunately, it does not receive much attention at the lower levels of administration (district and village) where the risks are greatest that ill-coordinated interventions by third parties, governmental or non-governmental, will undo what the SHPI has carefully helped to build up.
– The third proposal results from the need for inter-NGO collaboration at regional level and for geographical and functional specialization among them as

discussed before in Chapter 6, under 'Development dilemmas' of local NGOs. The SHPIs in the three countries could play a vanguard role in this respect, by initiating discussions on these matters in a more systematic way and at greater depth than could be done under the present study.

Instrument 7: Process extension and movement building

Action-reseachers from all three countries confirm the importance of movement building between SHOs, and also underwrite the proposition expressed in Chapter 3 (Instrument 7), that extension of the process to other villages and areas is primarily the responsibility and task of the SHO leadership. The question remains, how to put such broad principles into practice?

The APAEB case, Brazil
Concerning the structure of the SH movement there is the thorny question of horizontal versus vertical expansion. In the Brazilian case study a vertical regional structure, APAEB, was set up at an early stage to facilitate self-help activities at the grassroots within the 'comunidades'. Within the APAEB structure we see vertical and horizontal processes or motion, which have been schematized in Figure 12 below. On the left rectangular, motion is expressed in general terms; on the right, it is applied to the Brazilian case study.
In explanation of figure 12: the 'comunidades', SH groups from different localities, have created a regional organization, APAEB. This is an upward motion; the arrow goes upwards. APAEB sets up a wholesale service which is expressed by the horizontal arrow to the left. The management of the wholesale service entails a top-down motion; the arrow runs down vertically from wholesale service to the branches, the 'Postos'. The Postos are now in a situation where they have to submit themselves to the exigencies of 'sound business management'. At

Figure 12: Horizontal and vertical motion within a two-tier structure of SHOs*

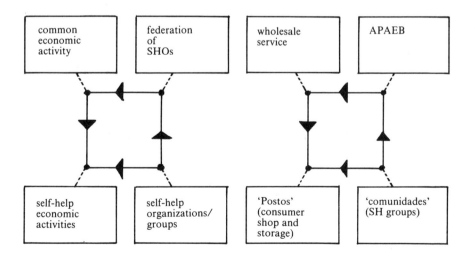

* Design adjusted from H. Desroche, 1985, p. 108.

the top, initiatives are taken which go downwards. Refusal to comply by the Postos may result in the whole organization going bankrupt. The Postos themselves, however, have been built and set up as a SH activity of the 'comunidades', which is expressed by the bottom arrow running from right to left.

Some APAEB leaders are of the opinion that APAEB as a people's *organization* has developed too fast (author's italics) but as an *economic enterprise*, having studied the economic results, we would say that it has not developed fast enough, because the combined turnover of the small number of branches (Postos) is still too small to support the overheads of the central service.

Recently, APAEB embarked upon a new commercial venture. A mobile shop visits ten villages which have no 'posto' (consumer shop) of their own. The mobile shop will help to boost APAEB turnover at a relatively low cost. But for the APAEB movement to take root in these same 'comunidades', APAEB will have to initiate other activities which can be managed by the groups themselves. The growth of the structure at an early stage in a vertical direction has given rise to problems in the economic and social spheres, which neither MOC staff nor APAEB leaders had anticipated. Now that the structure is there, it has to be managed and a certain amount of top-down initiatives, sanctioned by APAEB leadership, will have to be taken to ensure the economic survival of the organization.

The Thai and Indonesian cases
The policy used in structuring the movement of the two Thai DISACs, particularly the DISAC Chiengmai, is quite different. SHO activities are started on a very small scale by one or two groups in the same village (see the Ban Nua case). The activities of the 'core groups' serve as an example for other groups within the same village. Subsequently, a pioneer village like Ban Nua gets the status of 'mentor village'. Invitations are sent to neighbouring villages, often to relatives, to participate in local festivities. Visitors are brought face to face with the ongoing activities in the mentor village, and subsequently may ask delegates from the mentor village to come and explain the group activities in the visitors' villages. If the mentor village delegates are convinced of the seriousness of intent of the inhabitants of the other village, they make a gesture: in a traditional ceremony they provide the other village with some rice or two young calves as seed capital for a rice bank or buffalo bank.

In 1984, DISAC Chiengmai supported the setting up of an intergroup/inter-village Working Committee for Chomthong District, 'but the operation failed, the committee did not work' (p. 61, Thai report). One year later four SHOs with a genuine interest in inter-group collaboration together started a small savings scheme. At monthly meetings they exchanged experiences and discussed issues of common interest for possible joint action. By early 1986, their number had grown to eleven SHOs. A two-tier organization is slowly emerging.

122 The DISAC strategy is first to get the self-help idea and practice strongly rooted in the village communities, and to encourage inter-group collaboration only at a second stage, when the groups themselves feel the need for it. It builds on the social cohesion between villagers, which still exists in spite of the inroads made upon people's social behaviour and preparedness for collective action by the expansive capitalist economy.

The Indonesian case is again quite different. First, in the Indonesian context,

NGOs are not supposed to promote autonomous movements which pursue their own objectives of socio-economic change. They are accepted only in the complementary role of implementors of national development programmes (see for example Ismid Hadad, in Prisma, June 1983, p. 19). The political environment seems to some extent to be responsible for the flat structure of the Indonesian UB movement. As long as UBs continue to operate as isolated small groups spread over large geographical areas, they offer no real challenge to the existing government-controlled system of development institutions. But there are also factors inherent in the UBs as such, which further complicate the movement building process. After several prudent efforts and initiatives on the part of Bina Swadaya staff to elicit interest in inter-group meetings and activities, they could only conclude that the UB leaders themselves were simply not interested and preferred to go on their own way (Indonesian report, pp. 51-52). Unlike the situation in Brazil, where SHO leaders feel themselves part of a larger movement, UB leaders seem to have a narrower perspective focussed on the village and their own social position within it. Moreover, there are great differences in membership composition between UBs, and leaders find it difficult to appreciate that they have any common ground in economic matters.

Relationship between process extension and movement building
If one endorses the concept that process extension is mainly the responsibility of local leaders and can be done more effectively by them, then process extension and movement building become integrated and almost identical, the first laying the foundation for the second. With a view to raising the level of participation of local leaders, MOC encouraged the formation in two Districts of 'Grupos Populares de Acompanhamento'. These are in fact District level committees whose members have taken up the responsibility of acting as monitor to several new groups, in addition to the leadership function they already fulfil in respect of their own groups. It is a 'de facto' transfer of promotional functions from MOC staff to local leaders, who get compensated for their work input by payment of the equivalent of the minimum daily wage – a very modest amount for a leader. (MOC Annual Report 1985, p. 6).

The following lines of action might be considered by the respective SHPIs with regard to process extension and movement building:
– In the case of APAEB, supported by MOC, first, consolidation and rationalization of the present system of distribution of consumer goods at the Centre and at branch level, with the possible consequence that one or more consumer units will have to be closed; secondly, strengthening the basis of the movement by the encouragement of small-scale storage and processing activities and other collective initiatives which can be managed locally; in other words shifting the focus of process extension from regional to local level and from district towns to villages.*
– In the situation of the two DISACs in Thailand, there is need for a further concentration of promotional activities on selected smaller geographical areas (districts) and of 'mentor' villages within such areas, such as was tried out in

---

* The recommended policy would imply discontinuing the initiation of new economic ventures requiring large capital investments at 'Municipio' level. The existing mobile shop will function as a go-between between new villages where economic activities are undertaken which are economically viable and profitable from the beginning.

Chomthong District (the available number of field staff, however, is at present far too small to cope with the DISACs' ambitious development goals).
– Judging from the situation in Yogyakarta area, prospects for the building up of an authentic movement of UB groups in Indonesia do not seem particularly bright. It would be a more feasible alternative for some UBs which limit themselves to savings and loan business, to line up with the Indonesian national organisation of Credit Unions (CUCO-Indonesia). Implementation of such a policy, however, would call for closer ties between Bina Swadaya and the Indonesian Credit Union movement at national level, prior to greater coherence of action at field level.

Instrument 8: Monitoring and ongoing evaluation (MOE)

Monitoring and ongoing evaluation have been found to be the least developed instrument of the self-help promotion instrumentarium. The shortcomings of the present situation are detailed in all three country reports, and apply to all three levels where MOE is required: at the SHO level, at the level of SHPI-SHO interaction, and at the level of the interaction between the SHO/SHPI complex and other supporting institutions. This last type of interaction is still so poorly structured that MOE as a systematically organized regular practice and special form of inter-agency collaboration is still out of the question. In the following we shall therefore deal with the situation at the first two levels.

SHO-level
In none of the cases studied was a situation found capable of giving a knowledgeable and well-informed membership the opportunity to participate in MOE practice on a regular basis. A few very small groups in Thailand were the only exceptions. Two-weekly or monthly meetings at SHO level certainly facilitate holding leadership accountable for their deeds, but their dominant position needs to be counter-balanced by a more formalized mechanism, providing membership with the information they are entitled to, especially in respect of the use of money and distribution of benefits.
In Brazil, MOC action-researchers consider it of crucial importance that the present situation be remedied and that each SHO be assisted in the development of its own mechanism for assessing performance and progress of operations (MOC report, p. 65). In consequence, this aspect of MOC's promotional work will need much more attention than it was given in the past.
When groups are very small, such as in Ban Nua village, Thailand, a MOE mechanism may grow up by itself within such a group. But as SHO membership grows and operations become more complex, we normally see a development in the opposite direction: administrative powers tend to converge and be concentrated in the hands of a few persons. Bina Swadaya has introduced the REM system (Recording, Evaluation and Monitoring, see Indonesian report, p. 116 et seq.). The system aims at a regular flow of information from the UB groups upwards, via the field-workers and Field Offices, to the Central Office at Jakarta, and provides for a reflux of 'guidance' and 'feed back' from the Centre downwards to the UBs. The system as now practised has two main shortcomings:
– it does not work well because of shortage of qualified manpower at different levels and the long lines of communication (Indonesian report, p. 118);

– the present system lays the prime responsibility for MOE with the SHPI and not with SHO membership.

SHO-SHPI interaction
An important aspect of the MOE system is the participation of the SHOs in the assessment of the performance of their promoters, the SHPI. A classic way of doing this is to organize 'evaluation and planning' workshops, during which field staff and group representatives meet for a joint assessment of the overall situation, and discuss priorities of action for the future. All four SHPIs, MOC, Bina Swadaya and both the DISACs organize yearly workshops for this purpose. In the MOC case such meetings take place even more frequently. But, although considered helpful and necessary, such meetings in themselves do not allow 'to go beyond the level of what *appears* to be happening' ('ultrapassar o nivel do aparente').

What *really* happens under the apparent surface, and its impact on the day-to-day situation of SHO membership, remains rather vague or hidden. MOC in its latest development plan argues for a much more analytical approach and for not accepting the surface appearance as a confirmed fact. Monitoring and ongoing evaluation are basically analytical processes. They are easily overlooked in development practice which is characterized in many instances by haste and the day-to-day struggle for organizational survival. MOE is time-consuming. It also presupposes analytical interest and capacities on the part of its participants: SHO members, leaders, SHPI staff and other associated persons.

To strengthen such interest and capacities SHPIs might consider the following activities which, in content and orientation, take their direction from the experiences gathered during the present action-research:

– To conceive, design and implement an information system which will provide SHO members with sufficient up-to-date, easy-to-digest factual information and enable them to participate in MOE practice whithin their own organizations on a regular basis. The purpose is not to dream up a theoretically ideal system (and maximize participation) but to develop a low cost mechanism which will work in practice (in other words to *optimize* participation), and which logically fits in the earlier discussed system of functional education and mutual training (Instrument 3).

– To review regularly (monthly) and systematically at field office level, in consultation with SHO leadership, the SHPI's promotional practice (use and effectiveness of the other seven instruments); to consider realistically to what extent the responsibility for some promotional tasks could be transferred to 'local cadres' (people who originate from the ranks of SHO membership) at a proper indemnification and without overburdening them.

– To encourage and enable SHPI field staff: (a) to devote part of their time to action-research; more specifically, to select a number of villages where field-workers will try to assess the development impact of the SHOs on members and non-members, and deepen their insight into such crucial questions as: which categories of the village population benefit most from the self-help activities, what are the main problems of the disadvantaged section of the population which might be solved by group action, etc.; (b) to discuss with their colleagues, SHO leadership and members, the outcome of their investigations and their consequences for promotional practice, both informally and in more formal ways, during field workshops, preferably located in one of the 'lead' or 'mentor' villages.

9 Special aspects of self-help promotion

In this section we shall review two special aspects of self-help promotion which could not be dealt with in full in the foregoing parts of the report. Both are factors of considerable influence in the promotion and practice of self-help. Successively, we shall discuss:
– the holistic development approach as practised in some villages in Thailand;
– the relationship between local NGOs/SHPIs and foreign private co-financing agencies ('donor' NGOs).

The holistic development approach in Thailand

In Thailand a new development approach is rapidly gaining ground within NGO circles. We could call it a 'holistic' approach, since it emphasizes the basic unity and mutual interaction of different spheres of life: economic, political, social and cultural. It starts from the premise that the aim of development is the realization of certain basic values entrenched in Thai culture, which is predominantly Buddhist. The CCTD, a Catholic organisation, sees no fundamental difference, but rather congruence and complementarity between Buddhist and Christian inspired values, and endorses and actively promotes the holistic concept. Its dominant values and orientations are the pursuance of social justice and human dignity, with special concern for the weaker sections of society and the environment; the furtherance of solidarity and honesty at all levels; and greater freedom of choice for grassroot communities in determining development objectives and the means for achieving these. Widening the opportunities, creating space, for the realization and manifestation of such values is regarded as the only legitimate ground for any form of catalytic intervention by CCTD or DISACs, whether in the economic or other spheres of life. 'Economic activities which only propagate greed, and the kind of development which does not open up higher values, are no development' (Bishop Mansa, CCTD Workshop, personal notes).

What makes the approach interesting is not just its concept, but the way it is put into practice at village level. Villagers are encouraged to reflect on their own history and on the way the challenges and temptations posed by modern society, have changed their lives over the past decades. They weigh up the positive and negative points and on that basis plan for new activities, economic or otherwise. Development workers can play a role by helping to record that history, working in close cooperation with the 'organic intellectuals' in the village (Chattip, CCTD Workshop report, p. 4).* The direction chosen by the villagers on the basis of such analysis is normally to strengthen their capacity for food production and for the provision of other basic necessities, and thus to heighten their level of self-sufficiency at village level. One of the research villages, Ban Nua, has already gone some way in that direction, but other villages, such as those promoted by the North-East Community Development Workers Group, have already moved further ahead and accomplished a restructuring of the village economy. Such a restructuring may include: a rice bank to prevent the rice the villagers themselves would later need for their own consumption being sold to outside merchants, a medicine bank with an important section of herbal medicine; dyke construction for irrigated agricultural production and expansion of fishing grounds (primarily for enlarged village consumption, while the surplus can be sold); stamping rice in the traditional way so that the bran can be retained for feeding the pigs, rather than taking the whole crop to the rice mill; bee-keeping; sinking of tubewells for access to pure drinking water and making clay jars for its conservation; revival of home industries; common exploitation of a small collective field, the proceeds of which will feed the village budget, etc. In economic terms, the holistic approach aims to optimize resource utilization and allocation in a direction that will give priority to village consumption over production for the outside market. The changes over time in the production pattern of the villages' economy can be schematized as shown in figure 13.

Figure 13: Changes over time in production pattern: from self-subsistence to a balanced village economy

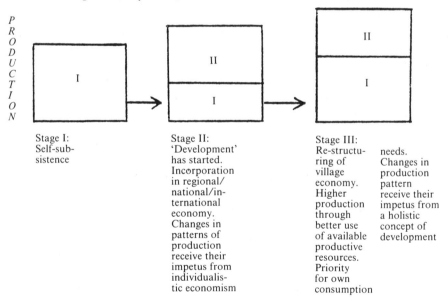

P
R
O
D
U
C
T
I
O
N

Stage I:
Self-sub-
sistence

Stage II:
'Development'
has started.
Incorporation
in regional/
national/in-
ternational
economy.
Changes in
patterns of
production
receive their
impetus from
individualis-
tic economism

Stage III:
Re-structu-
ring of
village
economy.
Higher
production
through
better use
of available
productive
resources.
Priority
for own
consumption

needs.
Changes in
production
pattern
receive their
impetus from
a holistic
concept of
development

I = Share of production used for exchange within the village or for home consumption
II = Share of production diverted to regional, national or international markets.

* The term 'organic intellectuals' as used by Chattip refers to a certain type of village inhabitant who possesses an analytical mind, combined with a sense of history. It has no connection with the level of school education. In Chapter 8 p. 108, the same concept was used in the narrower sense of young, socially-committed people, who are trained and guided to perform the double function of organic intellectual and development worker.

127

From a social point of view, the holistic approach is a deliberate attempt to counteract the disintegration of the village community. In Thailand, the bond and the relations within the community are still strong (Chattip, CCTD Workshop report, p. 3) and their strength is generally underestimated. Traditional ceremonies are important means to hold the communities together and offer an occasion par excellence to spur motivation and mobilize resources for self-help economic activities (e.g. rice donations to form the capital of a rice bank).

The holistic approach is a search for a more balanced pattern of development, for a new equilibrium in which the Buddhist temple and Buddhist (or Christian) teachings play an important role. It is definitely not, as its promoters never tire of repeating, a return to traditional society and to village autarky. It is a reaction against the one-sided sectoral approach of development technicians and bureaucrats who, due to their specialization, have become incapable of integrative thinking.

It aims at reaching a standard of living that is certainly adequate, but refuses to submit the villagers to forces beyond their control which draw them into a competitive race between individuals, which is of no lasting advantage. The approach also has a spiritual dimension. It is an attempt to remedy the prevailing imbalance between material growth and spiritual development.

This brings a new element to the self-help discussion: religion. Separating economic from spiritual matters is, from the holistic perspective, an artificial segmentation of spheres of life that will only create serious distortions (exploitation of men and nature resulting in poverty and ecological disaster). In this vision compulsory school education, the modern media and the capitalist system of production have eroded morality and discipline, and made people put their trust in the false prophecies of modern management and technology for the ultimate betterment of their lives. Restoring the Buddhist temple and teaching to their rightful place in shaping society implies, for example, that the monk be invited to meetings of self-help groups (Thai report, p. 65) and participate in the whole process of reflection and re-orientation of the economic, social, and cultural life of the village.

There are three more concepts central to the Thai version of the holistic approach which merit a short explanation:
– Intellectual self-reliance: This means that the village community develops its own vision of the desirable future, the 'imagined society'. (Apichart, personal discussion). A strategy is worked out, and economic and other activities are organized accordingly. When the villagers consider their own resource basis insufficient the pursuance of intellectual self-reliance also implies that the villagers acquire the necessary knowledge and skills to obtain access to additional resources; that they know from where, from whom and how to get the needed additional financial or technical inputs (a concept which runs parallel to that of 'Linkage building' discussed in Chapter 8). Support from outside is gladly accepted, provided it respects the villagers' autonomy of thinking and choice of priorities.
– The traditional development worker is ill-equipped to support this kind of process since he/she has been mis-educated and trained to view him or herself as a 'change agent' and not as a person to be changed through the interaction with villagers. Without an open mind and a willingness to change his/her perception

of reality, he/she will be unable to play his/her role adequately.

– The holistic approach attaches great value to self-employment within the setting of the nuclear family, the larger self-help group, or the village community. Wage labour is considered as a degrading condition. In many villages in Thailand (as well as elsewhere) wage labour is thought of as public recognition of the fact that one is not able to make oneself productive in one's immediate environment, or to make oneself useful by undertaking activities directly benefiting people towards whom one feels responsible.

In figure 14 the holistic approach has been schematized. For reasons of clarity, the 'negative' outputs of the 'imposing institutions' have been dramatized and confronted by the 'positive outputs' of the village level 'people's institutions'. Reality is of course more complex, and always a mixture of both. Further, the positive and negative outputs which come from different directions are at the same time inputs for a dynamic process of change. The synthesis of all these seemingly opposite forces from the bottom and the top should eventually make for a better society, in which social values and religious principles inspire and shape the economic institutions, and not vice versa.

Figure 14: Development and counter-development: an abstraction of the 'holistic approach' as practised in some Thai villages

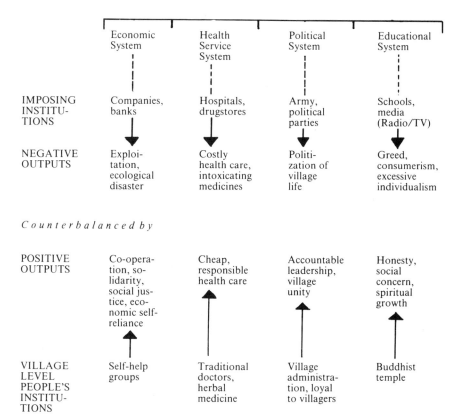

	Economic System	Health Service System	Political System	Educational System
IMPOSING INSTITU- TIONS	Companies, banks	Hospitals, drugstores	Army, political parties	Schools, media (Radio/TV)
NEGATIVE OUTPUTS	Exploi- tation, ecological disaster	Costly health care, intoxicating medicines	Politi- zation of village life	Greed, consumerism, excessive individualism

Counterbalanced by

	Economic System	Health Service System	Political System	Educational System
POSITIVE OUTPUTS	Co-opera- tion, so- lidarity, social jus- tice, eco- nomic self- reliance	Cheap, responsible health care	Accountable leadership, village unity	Honesty, social concern, spiritual growth
VILLAGE LEVEL PEOPLE'S INSTITU- TIONS	Self-help groups	Traditional doctors, herbal medicine	Village administra- tion, loyal to villagers	Buddhist temple

129

No matter how one views the holistic approach, as romantic illusionism or as a welcome correction to a one-sided economistic view of development, it has become part of reality in some Thai villages and is becoming increasingly popular in Thai NGO circles, not just as an idea but as a consistently pursued development praxis.

There are some obvious similarities between the Thai version of the holistic approach and the course of development as pursued by MOC, Brazil (see Chapter 6), particularly where MOC aims at integration of the 'religiosidade popular' in a liberating process of development (MOC's plan of work, 1986). The MOC view, however, carries more political overtones, which is typical of the Latin American situation.

In NGO circles in Indonesia there is also a latent sympathy for a more holistic approach to rural development as a correction to an orientation 'which places economics in command in fashioning development strategies' (Hendrata Lukas in Prisma, 1983, p. 21). But political circumstances at present do not seem to allow NGOs to adjust their strategies in line with a conception of socio-economic change which gives more room for village self-government.

Local NGOs and relations with foreign private co-financing agencies

The financing of programmes, the devolution of powers to the lower levels of the financing chain, the 'partnership' concept, and the role of foreign co-financing agencies in raising the consciousness of the general public in their home countries, all these are complex issues which call for much more elaborate treatment than can be given in this chapter. The lines of action suggested below should primarily be regarded as a logical follow-up to the earlier discussions on self-help promotion by local NGOs/SHPIs and as an input for further discussion. It should be borne in mind that it has been written mainly from the perspective of the participant local NGOs.

'Donor agencies think in terms of processes, but act in terms of projects' (Mauro Roberto da Costa Souza, personal conversation). There is no doubt that many donor NGOs are genuine in their concern to support self-sustaining processes of mobilization and organization at grassroot level. There is increasing doubt, however, about the effectiveness of the main instrument of international aid for achieving such a purpose: the 'project'.

Aid through projects does not seem to favour local initiative and local resource mobilization, nor to facilitate authentic grassroot level participation in the conception and planning of activities. 'Local leaders and field workers . . .

perceive projects as something decided in advance, not negotiable, and as an authoritarian and inflexible machine' (Lecompte, 1986, p. 9, author's translation). In Chapter 8, it was argued that self-help projects, like any other projects, especially when seeking capital investment, have to be well prepared and planned, and that local SHPIs have an important role to play in that process. There is nothing wrong with the project approach as such. In fact, the growing criticism in development circles on the project approach is not so much directed against the project concept itself, but against the way it is operated and embedded in an international system with its structural limitations hindering rather than faciliating people's participation.

The NGOs which participated in the present study also act within this international framework and, like many other NGOs, live 'from project to project'. Moneys arrive too late, provoking a near cash crisis, or have to be spent within certain time limits on projects which they have not been able to discuss in sufficient detail with the target population. If, on the other hand, NGO field workers have dutifully conducted such discussions, the delay in implementation while one has to wait for the cash to come from international sources, causes frustration and embarrassment.

A participatory approach requires the flexible use of funds and the assurance that the necessary financial assistance will be available in sufficient measure as and when the need arises. Even if some local NGOs have developed considerable skill in coping with the constraints imposed by the international system, this is no reason for not changing it where it could be simplified and gain in effectiveness. One of the more obvious inefficiencies of the present system is the time-consuming, detailed examination and appraisal of project budgets, which take place within the administrations of the donor NGOs, thousands of kilometers away from the site of implementation, and which interrupt or hinder a speedy follow-up to the earlier discussed processes of participatory research and planning. They also fail to take into account the impossibility of judging the economic, social, political and technical feasibility of village level micro-projects solely on the basis of project documents, however well prepared.

The earlier discussed changes of policy of local NGOs from service delivery to self-help promotion (Chapter 6), and of project holdership shifting from the local NGO to local SHOs, call for corresponding adjustments in the international system. One is that of more institutional support for those NGOs which really work with the poor and want to raise their level of competence and effectiveness. A second adjustment is the development of a mechanism whereby examination, appraisal and approval of economic projects can take place in the developing countries themselves and respond more quickly and adequately to specific needs of SHOs for technical (local consultancy) or financial assistance. Funding agencies which are reluctant to make that change and wish to preserve their powers of control and direction, in fact destroy the principles which they claim to cherish: grassroot level participation, mobilization of local resources, and creating opportunities for learning by doing.

The SHPIs which participated in the present study interact with a large number of donors: the field department of Bina Swadaya, Pusbinub, with sixteen donors, MOC with ten, and the umbrella organisation of the Diocesan Social Centres in Thailand, the CCTD, with six. Very understandably, they do not want to be dependent on a single foreign supporter but to divide their ties between several. This is a well known and widely practised way to avoid foreign agencies getting a too dominant grip on their organizations. 'Partner organization' is an expression popular in circles of donor NGOs to express their egalitarian stand in development cooperation as well as the permanency of their bond with the overseas party. But somehow it masks the de facto promiscuity at the recipient end, where the inflow of money is eased by courtesy of a bunch of 'partners' from different parts of the world.

However, the autonomy gained from working with several funding agencies is still relative. The *Indonesian report* warns explicitly against underestimating the impact of donor agencies on the policies and methods of work of local NGOs. 'Donor agencies... vary in terms of philosophy, ideology, objectives and strategy'. The result may be an odd mixture of concepts, strategies and projects. One project aims at dynamizing the village economy by creating new opportunities for individual middle-class entrepreneurs, while the other aims at a direct attack on rural poverty through the promotion of group effort. As a result, staff at field level get confused about what the target group is, whom they should support and how (Indonesian report, p. 125). Donor NGOs, so says the same report, also seem to feel attracted to larger NGOs which can absorb large amounts of aid, and tend to neglect the contribution smaller NGOs could make by being less bureaucratic and closer to the target population.

The *Thai report* is critical of the rigidity of donors regarding the magnitude of the counterpart contribution they ask for. The Thai researchers endorse wholeheartedly the principle of a contribution from own resources, but there are cases where this may inhibit the poorest in the village from participating (Thai report, p. 84). The foreign NGO, of necessity, has too little knowledge of the local situation to be able to judge whether a contribution from own resources is substantial by local standards or not.

In the Thai action-researchers' perception, present procedures as applied by international NGOs are an institutionalized expression of distrust. If collaboration remains limited to the provision of money, it has no intrinsic value and would be better stopped. Crucial to them is that development cooperation should contribute to heightening the awareness and widening the horizons of all partners involved, including the general public in the 'donor' countries.

The international aid system is in fact an easy target for criticism and one could go on adding to the list of shortcoming and inconsistencies. More relevant would be to give consideration to concrete measures which would improve its functioning, since international financial support will presumably continue for many years to come.

Even though this study was principally concerned with the promotion of economic activities by SHPIs, its findings also have implications for the international system. In the following some broad orientations for reform are suggested which need further consideration and articulation in the situation of each country and individual SHPI:

– To make the system more effective, particularly for self-help promotion at grassroot level, donor NGOs must be prepared to delegate authority for project appraisal and approval of economic projects to local institutions, based in the developing country (preferably not the SHPI itself: see below); in other words a transfer of the 'intake' of economic projects from the donor country to the developing country. The first steps taken in this direction – the mini-fund programme of CERIS (supported by Cebemo), and the KSK programme of Bina Swadaya – need further elaboration. However, where the local institution has reason to fear that it could be subjected to political pressure and interference in its decision-making, it may agree that the foreign agency should retain the ultimate power of approval and thus act as a scapegoat for the local institution, if necessary.

– In line with the earlier recommendation (Chapter 8) of a separation between promotional work and financing, foreign agencies should assist in building-up a suitable institutional framework in developing countries for project appraisal and approval, and look for alternative ways of chanelling finances, for example:

a. an agreement with an existing local financial institution on special savings and credit facilities for local SHOs (e.g. a commercial bank, sympathetic to self-help promotion, assisted by a special committee for project appraisal with NGO representation);

b. a special branch within a national umbrella-type of NGO, which is not itself directly involved in self-help promotion (e.g. a special section within the CCTD appraising projects of SHOs supported by DISACs, with participation of local banking institutions on the loan appraisal committee);

c. the Bina Swadaya formula of a special department within the organization itself for handling requests from SHOs for project financing, while at the same time keeping promotional and financial functions separated at field level, i.e. field workers will no longer be used as loan officers and local banks will be used for the forwarding of finances to self-help groups (the system has been planned as such but has yet to be put into practice).

– Foreign agencies should be more active in facilitating the building up of a capacity for self-help promotion with an explicit poverty focus within their overseas partner organizations. In practice this will mean broad 'programme' support. This support will be used not directly to finance economic activities, but indirectly to develop a self-help promotion instrumentarium that derives its orientation and direction from the suggested lines of action, set out in the previous sections of this report. Such programme support should include regular grants over a long period of time, from which the SHPI can cover the salaries of its field workers, travelling costs, special education and training activities, as well as the use of local consultancy for micro-project preparation and other technical assistance which SHOs may need in the course of project implementation.*

– Foreign agencies need to further refine and expand their financial instrumentarium to be able to provide financial assistance which is well tuned to the local situation. Such an instrumentarium may comprise:

a. incentive deposits: a fund placed directly with a local financial institution which can be used to provide small subsidies (seed-money) to facilitate the start of micro-projects with an explicit poverty focus;

b. placement with a local financial institution of a revolving credit fund for on-lending to SHOs;

c. collateral deposits which would help to cover part of the risks involved when lending to SHOs;

d. equity participation of donor NGOs in local banks with the prospect of transferring their shares to SHOs or SHO Federations in due course.

(The gist of these recommendations have been derived from the S 24/ES 31 study, Osner et al., 1984).

– In figure 15 (p. 134), a tentative model is suggested for the flow of finances from a foreign private co-financing agency to a developing country. It is in accordance with the earlier recommendations. Its main characteristics are:

a. the funding agency (e.g. a 'donor' NGO) provides long-term institutional

---

* In practice, this is already done by some foreign private agencies, but the broadness and freedom of choice as to the ultimate allocation of monies varies very much from case to case.

Figure 15: Tentative model of a new system for structuring money transfers from a foreign private co-financing agency to a developing country

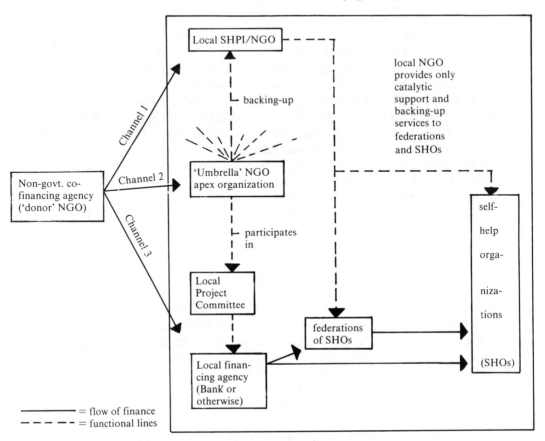

Developing country

Local SHPI/NGO

local NGO provides only catalytic support and backing-up services to federations and SHOs

backing-up

Channel 1

Channel 2

'Umbrella' NGO apex organization

Non-govt. co-financing agency ('donor' NGO)

Channel 3

self-

help

orga-

niza-

tions

participates in

Local Project Committee

federations of SHOs

(SHOs)

Local financing agency (Bank or otherwise)

————— = flow of finance
– – – – – = functional lines

support to the local SHPI/NGO for preparation and implementation of specific programmes. (Channel 1);

b. umbrella organizations of local NGOs/SHPIs (such as CCTD, Thailand; CERIS, Brazil) streamline interaction between the foreign agency and specific

134 categories of local SHPIs/NGOs with a regional focus (e.g. DISACs in Thailand). For this and other back-up functions, the umbrella organizations are given institutional support (Channel 2);

c. project appraisal and approval are carried out in the developing country by a local Project Committee. Location and composition of the Committee are dependent upon the level of involvement of local banks and the stage of development of the SHO movement;

d. finance for important economic projects is channelled through local financing agencies (Channel 3). If Channel 3 is impracticable, Channels 3 and 2 may have to be combined into one. When institutional development in the developing country is still at a very low stage, the three financial streams may have to be merged for practical reasons. There are many variations on the above which are both possible and desirable. The translation of the general principle 'project appraisal and approval in the developing country' into practice will take time. There will be many technical constraints to overcome, but perhaps the major one is attitudes.

10 Summary and main conclusions

Organization

The study initiated by Cebemo was carried out at four locations in three countries: one in Brazil, one in Indonesia and two smaller sites in Thailand. It was carried out by *local NGOs*, partner-organizations of Cebemo, which in the present study have been termed *Self-Help Promotion Institutions (SHPIs)*.

Self-help promotion

'Promotion' refers to the development task these SHPIs have set themselves, namely to facilitate the emergence and foster the functioning of cooperative-type organizations at grassroots level, known as Self-Help Organizations (SHOs). A SHO is an autonomous organization which subsists on the contributions of its members in terms of entrepreneurial skills, labour, capital or land. SHOs are considered a means of achieving self-reliance, which has been defined as the condition whereby the poor majority no longer depend on the benevolence, initiatives and skills of third parties (outsiders) to secure their interests.

Self-assessment by local NGOs

The present study was organized as a self-assessment of the effectiveness of their work methods by the participating local NGOs. In this way it tried to circumvent the classical dichotomy between researchers and practitioners, ensure the relevance of its findings, and heighten the likelihood of follow-up action. Such an approach stands to reason when the major objective of the whole study is to increase the effectiveness of local NGOs in supporting the economy of the poor (see Chapter 2). The kind of approach followed has brought about some limitations as to validity and representativity of findings (see Chapter 3) but these are offset by important gains in terms of contributions to operational theory and practicability of findings for the local NGOs concerned. In reviewing the study's results, it is convenient to distinguish: (a) the outcome of the research process as a tool for organizational change, and (b) study findings. The remainder of this concluding chapter will be devoted to findings, except for the next paragraph, which will summarize the outcome of the process.

The outcome of the research process

– In the case of MOC, Brazil, the study has produced at all levels a heightened awareness of the vulnerability of the small farmer movement (APAEB) under whose banner a series of activities of doubtful economic viability had been undertaken. It has provoked a change of policy as to location and selection of new activities as well as generated new initiatives for the consolidation of existing ones.
– In the Bina Swadaya case, Indonesia, the study has helped the realization that a more 'target group'-oriented approach is needed for the SHPI to meet its social development objectives, and a new programme has been designed which will test out such an approach.
– In the Thai case, it has helped to conceptualize and formulate a methodology of SH promotion which has had a certain amount of success in two Dioceses (DISACs). The research material and experience are being used to feed an ongoing discussion among development organizations affiliated to the national organization CCTD.
– At the Cebemo level, the study has activated a policy discussion, still in progress, on desirable changes in patterns of interaction between NGO foreign financing agencies and local NGOs in general, and in modalities of financing in particular. In this respect, too, the 'systems thinking' has helped to ensure that a factor with such great influence on the direction and nature of grassroots level promotional work is given due consideration. Cebemo will also be enlarging the scope of the self-help promotion discussion at national and international level.

A systems approach

The primary stress of this study was on the role local NGOs play in creating and maintaining a suitable environment for SHO performance. The body of knowledge related to this specific task can be classified under eight major categories, termed self-help promotion instruments (see Figure 3, p. 29). Together, the instruments form an interlocking and interacting complex of activities; they are at the centre of the conceptual framework which has served as a basis for the organization of the present study. Instruments, SHPIs (local NGOs), other supporting institutions and SHOs are the component parts of the 'Self-Help Promotion System'. This system, designed in the early stages of the study, was discussed and adjusted as the study progressed, and finally experienced as a useful and practical tool for the analysis of reality.

It may still need some adjustment in wording. For example the term 'target population' is somewhat of a misnomer since it does not fit well into a process in which the rural poor are the chief actors. In such a situation the role of local NGOs could be better described as 'con-motion' (moving with) rather than 'pro-motion'. The term 'self-help' is also not free from ambiguity when applied in the local cultural context (see Chapter 4). Yet, as a whole, we may say that the framework and related concepts have stood the test of relevance for the analysis of practice.

137

The eight instruments reviewed

For any organization, the mere statement of noble objectives will not guarantee their fulfilment. Development agencies are no exception, and this includes NGOs which aim to contribute to a more just, egalitarian society by promoting different sorts of economic activities through Self-Help Organizations. One of the main conclusions of the present action-research is, that the NGOs acting as SHPIs seem to operate under a number of constraints, sometimes of external origin, sometimes self-imposed, which leave them insufficient time to develop a clear and comprehensive strategy of SH promotion and, by implication, make it a difficult task to achieve the above stated development goal.

In the following we shall consider what positive elements and what gaps and shortcomings the action-researchers, through study and dialogue, have been able to identify in the SHPIs' past and present 'instrumentarium', which have a direct bearing on the operations and performance of SHOs. Later in this chapter we shall consider how some of the constraints might possibly be removed by changes in policy and practice at SHPI or international level. Some of the most important lessons are the following:

Instrument 1: Identification of the 'target population' and groups
In SH promotion the danger of by-passing the poor, or the poorer sections among the poor is great, especially when activities centre upon economic issues. Without proper identification of the target population in the village setting, field staff may simply be unaware of the fact that the poor majority is not, or hardly, represented among the SHO membership (particularly in the Indonesian case). Target population identification can be greatly facilitated by the use of appropriate indicators. Landholding criteria are often used but they are in themselves insufficient. Indicators are highly contextual (housing, food habits) and there are no fixed rules on how to develop them. In the Thai experience the villagers themselves, members of a 'core group', can play a key role in identification of the poorer strata of the village community.

Instrument 2: Participatory research and planning
It was also found that SHPI staff in general lacked in-depth knowledge of the socio-economic conditions of the disadvantaged category of the rural poor. If these are not thoroughly understood, SHPI staff are unlikely to be very effective in generating economic activities essential for the improvement of such conditions. There are various ways of carrying out a social analysis at village level. Where it was done under the present study, the unanimous conclusion was that this kind of up-front input is well worth the time spent on it. The Brazilian and Indonesian case studies showed how crucial it is to assess the feasibility of an economic activity in its various dimensions: economic, technical, social, political as well as operational. If the latter aspect is neglected, one runs the risk of encouraging and supporting activities which go beyond the capacity for self-administration and management of the SHO leaders (Brazil in particular). It would seem better policy to adjust the size of operations to the available management capacities rather than trying to solve the dearth of managerial skill by substantial input from skilful outsiders. The transfer of administrative and managerial functions from a local NGO to SHO local leaders or staff is a painful process, that often does not work. There should be no illusions about the

138

difficulties of integrating the poorest of the poor, viz. the (near-) landless, into a participatory process. They have less time to spare for group discussions and are normally less vocal. They may also feel ashamed to acknowledge the reality of their condition (Indonesia).

Instrument 3: Education and mutual training
Education and training activities, especially when conducted in an atmosphere remote from day-to-day village reality (Training Centres), were found to be largely ineffective and to some extent counter-productive (Thailand, Indonesia). Village based gatherings offer better opportunities for a two-way process of 'knowledge sharing and generation' and are less costly.

Instrument 4: Mobilization and provision of resources
The provision of external resources, in particular the availability of credit and subsidies, may undermine the self-help orientation and may in fact act as a disincentive to local resource mobilization. The Thai researchers warned against 'exploitative' resource provision and the agressive policies of development banks, which push credit needs to levels where farmers lose their autonomy, and finally have to subject their economies to bank policies. The case of Ban Nua village (Thailand) shows that a self-help movement at village level can start without material support from outsiders. More consideration should be given by SHPIs to ways and means of mobilizing local resources which the poor have and from which they are willing to contribute. The spending pressure of the large foreign aid organizations, transmitted to governmental and non-governmental local agencies, however, is a major external factor which may inhibit the pursuit of a consistent policy of local resource mobilization in rural areas.

Instrument 5: Management consultancy
Once economic activities have started ('project implementation'), proper monitoring of financial performance is impossible without a suitable bookkeeping system (Indonesia and Brazil). And by disregarding depreciation of donor-financed assets and various kinds of 'hidden subsidies', dependence on donor money is easily masked while the ordinary SHO members live under the illusion that their operations are showing a surplus (Brazil). The good performance of Indonesian UBs in savings and loan operations contrasts with their poor record in respect of other economic activities (processing, marketing). Savings and loan transactions seem easier to manage, and the introduction of this type of cooperative to places where it does not yet exist (Brazil), merits serious consideration.

Instrument 6: Movement building and process extension
When the promoted self-help organizations are scattered over many villages and situated at great distances from each other, it becomes very difficult to facilitate the build-up of a self-help movement, viz. a network of interacting mutually supportive SHOs from different villages. The 'butterfly' approach is not very appropriate to movement building. For the process to become a movement which stretches out beyond the narrow confines of a village, SHPIs would do better to concentrate on smaller areas and select so-called 'core' or 'mentor' villages from which the process can spread to neighbouring localities, a policy deliberately pursued by some Thai NGOs.

Instrument 7: Linkage building

SHPIs have a tendency to regard the SHOs they have promoted as 'their groups', while SHOs on their part tend to push the promoting institution into a 'godfather role', which is contrary to the self-help philosophy. Hence the importance of building links so that the SHOs, as autonomous organizations, are free to approach the non-governmental and governmental agencies which they feel can best serve their interests in certain fields. Over the past few years, SHPIs (Brazil and Thailand) have put greater effort into assisting SHOs to raise their claim-making capacities vis-à-vis government authorities and thus to gain access to their legitimate share of public service facilities. This represents an important shift in promotion policies.

Instrument 8: Monitoring and ongoing self-evaluation

The reports from the three countries repeatedly stress the need for a more regular and systematic assessment of strategy, working methods and performance, and for an in-built feed-back mechanism, which at present is either non-existent or not functioning properly.

This latter instrument, i.e. monitoring and ongoing self-evaluation, is considered so crucial that all the SHPIs which participated in the study view the building up of such a mechanism within their organizations as a priority matter and the main focus for follow-up action. The main thrust of the recommended lines of action goes in two directions:

– to raise the level of participation in the administration of instruments so that promotion increasingly becomes self-promotion;

– to develop a methodology for self-help promotion which must not be allowed to suffer from the passion for more projects and quick implementation.

The Brazilians call this kind of hurried development activism 'tarefismo'. It is widespread in NGO circles as well as elsewhere. It may facilitate the absorption of donor money but not the development of a consistent strategy. Local NGOs/ SHPIs of good international reputation are much shorter of breathing space to develop an adequate instrumentarium for SH promotion than of additional finance for new economic projects.

SHPI-SHO relationships: breaking with the 'father knows best' tradition

Over the past ten years there has been a change of perspective within the four SHPIs as to their role in development. But under the pressures of day-to-day work they have not been able to carry this through fully in promotional practice. It is more and more realized that the real knowledge about what should be done and can be done in the field of economic activities is primarily located with the rural populations themselves, and that the outsiders' role should be reduced to a supportive function from the very beginning of the operation. Recognizing this fact has been difficult for all those staff who have been educated and trained in the 'father knows best' tradition.

It would be equally wrong to go to the other extreme and deify local knowledge and wisdom to the extent of leaving no role for the outside promoter other than as the occasional provider of money.

What is important is the quality of SHPI-SHO interaction. SHOs need assistance in financial appraisal, while SHPIs need the SHOs' input for a balanced judgement of overall feasibility, especially of social and operational feasibility.

SHPI relations with other supporting organizations

A single SHPI cannot be expected to possess all the knowledge and skills necessary to support, with sufficient confidence, local SHOs in the broad range of economic and non-economic activities they may wish to undertake. Hence the importance of the earlier mentioned linkage building, not only between SHOs and other support agencies but also at regional and district level between the various development agencies. The differing policies pursued and work methods practised by non-governmental and governmental agencies – all eager to expand their zones of influence as well as their staff – create a climate of confusion at village level. Strategy development implies a serious effort on the part of the SHPI to bring about a form of harmony in its development approach and the division of functions between various agencies.

There is an ongoing debate among foreign governmental and non-governmental agencies as to whether or not NGOs in developing countries should be encouraged to seek collaboration with local governments. Both SHPIs and SHOs, at least in the cases studied, seem to come to terms with this problem each in their own way. The general thrust is that of a growing collaboration between the NGO sector and governmental bodies. The latter are politically powerful but at the same time feel powerless to halt the rising tide of rural poverty.

Separation of self-help promotion and banking functions

Under present conditions, a lot of the SHPIs' attention and energy is devoted to the role they should probably *not* play, that of a financing agency which acts as an intermediary in the flow of resources from donor agencies to the local SHOs. This leaves them insufficient attention and energy to devote to the role they *should* play: a catalytic and supportive role in a series of interconnected processes at grassroot level such as mobilization of local resources, organization of the rural poor, and identification and preparation of economic activities which primarily strengthen the latter's economic and social position. A clear separation between promotional and banking functions is therefore recommended.

Characteristic features of an effective SHPI

The scope of the present study does not permit any definite conclusions on the essential structural and functional features of an effective SHPI. Indications, however, go in the following direction: for self-help promotion the most effective SHPI is probably a small one whose staff can function as a single team with a (sub) regional focus (approximately 10 to 20 persons); it has a high degree of autonomy in deciding its policies, but at the same time forms part of a network of support organizations which complement – if need be on a consultancy basis – the facilities and services which a small SHPI is unable to provide. NGOs in which the field-worker is relegated to the position of the lowest lackey in a bureaucratic hierarchy are unsuitable as SHPIs. In short: for a NGO small is beautiful, but not too small.

Financial self-reliance for SHPIs

Local NGOs acting as SHPIs are faced with a dilemma when they are pressed by donor agencies to become self-reliant, in other words, to create their own sources of revenue in order to prevent continuing financial dependence on the donor agency. The Indonesian Bina Swadaya organization is a typical case in point. Since it is difficult to make money out of the poor, it is necessary to undertake and maintain projects which generate income from transactions with a more affluent middle class clientèle. When a local NGO/SHPI has become an entrepreneur and conducts its own business in trade, processing or otherwise, the organization is easily distracted from its main function of self-help promotion. However, the alternative course of action, namely to concentrate on self-help promotion and refrain from activities which feed the SHPI's own budget, will inevitably result in lasting dependence on foreign agencies and local donations. One may ask whether, for a SHPI, there is any golden mean between self-help promotion and helping itself. This study does not answer that question but illustrates the dilemma local NGOs are facing, the full dimensions of which not all foreign agencies appear to recognize.

Positive aspects of SHO performance

Given the restrictive circumstances under which the SHPI/SHOs complex operates, it is remarkable what it has been able to achieve in terms of SHO efficiency and development performance. In discussing performance one should be aware that SHO members may have quite different criteria for utility assessment and development impact from those applied and perceived by development agencies. As emphasized in the *Indonesian study*, what in project documents may be termed as 'production loans' are normally used for different purposes, and this for good reasons. Borrowers, quite rationally, use the additional liquidity to purchase goods or services which they feel they need most. Defying the logic of conventional thinking, such a diversion from official rules does not engender default. The SHOs promoted by the Bina Swadaya, called UBs, display a remarkable repayment discipline and a high degree of organizational autonomy. Members also save regularly and substantially (see Chapter 7).

The members of the SHOs promoted in the *Thai villages* give proof of a capacity for reflection which makes them show concern not only for their own future but also for that of their children and the development process as a whole. In their view, the course which 'development' has taken so far has inflicted a lot of damage on village society, and to counteract this, a more balanced process of change must be organized. The promotion of self-help must be seen in that perspective. The 'holistic' approach which in recent years has become a fashionable topic of international discussion, is already practised in some Thai villages with the support of local NGOs (see Figure 14, p. 127). Economic activities are not valued 'per se' but only to the extent that they contribute to the achievement of a religiously inspired value system. Where this is practised, the villagers pursue a policy of increased economic and intellectual self-reliance which makes them less dependent on the 'feeding-bottles' of development agencies. An important index to their economic self-reliance is the reserve funds which the older groups over the years have accumulated (see Chapter 7). The Thai study, although limited in scope, seems to offer the hopeful perspective that the slow building-up of an associative economy at village level may gradually stop the ongoing process of pauperization which strikes large sections of the rural populace. In all cases, the poor were found to be over-burdened by a combination of time-consuming household and income-earning occupations. Not suprisingly, the Thai landless population as the main benefit of having a rice bank of their own mentioned the fact that they now have to spend less time in searching for sources of credit at acceptable rates.

The economic activities of the *Brazilian APAEB organization* bolster up a political struggle. So far this regional organization has managed to survive in a capitalistic environment by capitalizing on the 'human factor', particularly the commitment of its leadership, and financially, it must be admitted, on substantial donor support. If it succeeds, it will set an example to the many other Brazilian 'people's organizations' which tend to give one-sided emphasis to political 'people's education' ('educação popular').

One cannot easily overestimate the economic impact of a village consumer shop on a landless labouring household, bringing down consumer prices by nearly one third and saving numerous trips to town (see Chapter 7).

The impact assessments undertaken under the present study, admittedly, have not gone much further than a first exploration. But still they have had the merit of opening up some new unexpected vistas of what matters most from the poor's perspective in terms of social and economic change. In most studies and project documents, self-help is emphasized as a means for the rural poor to become more productive. However important this might be, from the perspective of the SHO members who have participated in this study, the main advantages lay in another direction, namely, that by group action they had to *pay less*, for credit, for consumer articles (including food), for seeds, for agricultural implements and for processing facilities, and also saved time and energy. By permitting the poor to bring down their costs of production, and to spend less on the satisfaction of their basic needs as consumers, a socially organized associative economy is also likely to have an indirect, positive impact on levels of production. However, the scope of the present study did not allow confirmation or otherwise of such impact.

The cultural dimension

The Thai study with its emphasis on values and morality has brought a new element to the self-help discussion: religion. Religion as an element of culture is under-studied in the literature on people's participation and self-help. Objectively, one has to admit that separating religion from economic development and its relegation to the cultural sphere of life is certainly not the outcome of a process of 'people's participation'. Rather it is a reflection of the hidden development ideology of the official development agencies, which is technocratic and secular. Culture, including its religious dimensions, seems to be the keyword in filling the gap between the technocrat's vision of reality and people's aspirations for positive changes. Field-workers should first seek out the sources of wisdom that exist within local cultures, without assuming that their own technical knowledge will provide the answer to a given need.

Horizontal or vertical expansion of economic activities?

Another question to which the action-researchers addressed themselves was in which direction self-help organization should be strengthened, horizontally or vertically. In western countries over the past decade, the cooperative sector has shown a rapid evolution in the vertical direction. There are developing countries where this pattern has been followed, with the result that, on the whole, cooperatives have failed to serve the poor. The present study is one of many to illustrate that small self-administered village-level micro-projects can produce substantial benefits (savings and credit groups, storage of food grains, collective gardens, small village-level processing industries, etc.). Such projects have the advantage of providing a foundation for the subsistence economy of the poor, and improving their bargaining position when producing for the market. They require, in general, very modest amounts of investment. The poor majority has more to gain from the multiplication of this kind of small-scale activity than from the more complex undertakings which operate at levels beyond their control. This does not alter the fact that the smaller self-help units can provide the bricks for vertical structures, but such inter-group and inter-village forms of enterprise should grow in a natural way, as and when the need for this arises. They should not be artificially forced by injections of capital arising from the spending urge of funding agencies or the empire-building aspirations of local NGOs. Most of the financial needs of SHOs can be met by small amounts of local currency.

Shortcomings of the present system of international funding

Having analysed the interaction between organizations at different levels, the study demonstrates that the present system, characterized by project financing, offers in itself no guarantee that the poor majority will be the ultimate beneficiaries. If they do benefit, it is due primarily to the commitment, insight and intuition of the local field-worker in combination with a certain amount of luck. The present system allows local NGOs to survive and subsist through financing on a 'project to project' basis. Under this system, they will gather a lot of experience, but will also remain short of time to harness such experience and develop a consistent strategy and methodology of intervention. NGOs in general, and not only those which undertook this study, are ill-equipped to promote economic activities. They lack time for careful social and economic analysis, for the necessary profound dialogue with leaders, and for cross-checking information through direct contacts with the ordinary members, the 'followers'. They also lack sufficient manpower and expertise to provide the required back-up services in such fields as project appraisal, bookkeeping and financial management. When the economic activities of self-help organizations remain simple and small-scale, the need for such back-up services is also small, but it still exists and remains

144 largely unsatisfied.

The prevalent situation of a multitude of funding agencies, all eager to finance concrete, tangible undertakings (grain mills, consumer shops, pumps, etc.) provides no encouragement to local NGOs to develop an adequate instrumentarium to sustain the dynamics of self-help. And without such tools, local NGOs cannot effectively play their role as SHPIs. If on the other hand, SHPI capacity in this respect can be enhanced, the pattern of financing will need considerable change. For it is clear that if self-help promotion is effective, local NGOs will be able, to a large extent, to satisfy their capital needs from collective savings or, if these are insufficient, from direct approaches to local financing institutions (e.g. banks).

This is not to argue in favour of giving local NGOs, acting as SHPIs, blank cheques for strategy development. Rather it is a plea for broader programme support while maintaining accountability for actual use of funds.

Another anomaly in the present system is that the detailed examination and appraisal of project budgets still takes place within the bureaucracies of the foreign funding agencies, thousands of kilometers away from the sites of implementation. This task should be delegated to one or more institutions in the developing country itself, where there is much easier access to up-to-date and precise information on local circumstances, and the possibility of direct consultation with the 'project holders' (in self-help promotion, the SHOs are the project holders, not the local NGO/SHPI which supports the process). The functions performed by a body like CERIS in Brazil go some way in that direction.

The responsibilities of SHPIs

Local NGOs, acting as SHPIs, have their own responsibilities. They must not only respond to the requests, demands, reactions and claims of self-help groups, but on their own initiative take action to ensure that the poor majority benefits from group activities in an equitable manner and is involved in the process of group formation. A cultural factor which was found important in all three countries – and which impinges heavily on member participation and the development performance of SHOs – is the dominant position of the village leadership in the decision-making process. Support from local leaders is necessary, but at the same time it constitutes a barrier between SHPI staff and the poor majority which the SHPI aims primarily to serve. SHPIs have the dual task of constantly reminding local leaders of their responsibility for the involvement and well-being of the more disadvantaged sections of the population, while at the same time developing a mechanism for the occasional crossing of that barrier to check whose interests the SHOs are actually serving.

In the Thai conception, field-workers should follow the line of thinking of those villagers who take a more holistic view of development. Without this the ethical and moral aspects of development work are likely to be disregarded, and with this the meaning of development.

The responsibilities of private foreign funding agencies

Similar reasoning applies to non-governmental foreign funding agencies ('donor NGOs'): if they are to contribute to the socio-economic emancipation of the poor majority in the developing countries, they should not merely respond to requests for financing from their overseas partners. By joint studies and dialogue, they should more vigorously pursue a policy which aims at building up, within the partner organizations, a capacity for self-help promotion with a more explicit focus on poverty alleviation, both in its technical and ethical dimensions. Once that capacity exists, there is no reason why foreign agencies should continue to maintain their dominant position in project appraisal and approval procedures. A larger devolution of powers to the developing country will also free the 'partnership' relationship between foreign and local NGOs from much of its present ambiguity.

Appendices

Appendix 1: List of abbreviations

APAEB (Brazil)	Associação dos Pequenos Agricultores do Estado da Bahia (The Association of Small Producers of the State of Bahia)
BAAC (Thailand)	Bank for Agriculture and Agricultural Cooperatives
BS (Indonesia)	Bina Swadaya (Agency for Community Self-Reliance Development), Jakarta
CCTD (Thailand)	Catholic Council of Thailand for Development, Bangkok
CEBEMO	Katholieke Organisatie voor medefinanciering van ontwikkelingsprogramma's (Catholic Organization for the joint financing of development programmes), Oegstgeest, The Netherlands
CERIS (Brazil)	Centro de Estatistica Religiosa e Investigações Sociais, Rio de Janeiro
COPAC	Committee for the Promotion of Aid to Cooperatives, FAO Building, Rome
CUCO (Indonesia)	Credit Union Coordination
DISAC (Thailand)	Diocesan Social Action Centre
DSE	Deutsche Stiftung für internationale Entwicklung (German Foundation for International Development), Federal Republic of Germany
HKTI (Indonesia)	Himpunan Kerukunan Tani Indonesia (All-Indonesia Farmers' Association)
IPP (Indonesia)	Ikatan Petani Pancasila (Pancasila Farmers' Movement)
KAS	Konrad Adenauer Stiftung (Konrad Adenauer Foundation), Federal Republic of Germany
KSK (Indonesia)	Kredit Setia Kawan; BS-administered 'solidarity credit' programme
KUD (Indonesia)	Koperasi Unit Desa (Village level Cooperative Unit). Government-supervised programme
LPSM (Indonesia)	Lembaga Pengembangan Swadaya Masyarakat (Agency for the Development of Self-Help and Self-Reliance). Official name of Indonesian NGOs

MOC (Brazil)	Movimento de Organização Comunitaria
MOE	Monitoring and ongoing evaluation
NGO	Non-Governmental Organization
NESDB (Thailand)	National Economic and Social Development Board
OECD	Organization for Economic Cooperation and Development
PKK (Indonesia)	Pembinaan Kesejahteraan Keluarga (Family Welfare Movement). Women's groups operating under the supervision of the Ministry of Home Affairs
PUSBINUB (Indonesia)	Pusat Pembinaan Usaha Bersama; Bina Swadaya's Centre for Pre-cooperative Development
SHO	Self-Help Organization
SHPI	Self-Help Promotion Institution
TCDC	Technical Cooperation between Developing Countries
UB (Indonesia)	Usaha Bersama (Collective Action); Bina Swadaya-supported savings and credit pre-cooperative
YSTM (Indonesia)	Yayasan Sosial Tani Membangun (Peasant Socio-Economic Development Foundation)

Appendix 2: Conversion tables

Brazil
1 hectare	=	2.3 tarefa
US$ 1	=	Crz 13.77

Indonesia
US$ 1	=	Rp 1,124

Thailand
1 rai	=	0.16 hectare
	=	0.4 acre
1 thang	=	15 kg.
US$ 1	=	Baht 26

Appendix 3: Glossary of local terms

Brazil
Assistencialismo	–	A kind of aid which makes the aid-receiving party dependent on the aid-giving party
Caixa	–	Informal thrift and credit group
Casa de farinha	–	Cassava mill
Fazendeiros	–	Large-scale livestock farmers
Municipio	–	Administrative area, comparable to a District
Mutirão	–	Traditional cooperation
Posto	–	Consumer shop
Sindicatos	–	Rural Trade Unions

Indonesia

Abangan	–	Practitioner of traditional Javanese religion
Arisan	–	Traditional savings and credit association
Dasa wisma	–	Neighbourhood group
Kabupatan	–	Administrative unit: district
Kelurahan	–	Administrative unit: cluster of villages
Padi gogo	–	Dry field rice
Pancasila	–	The official ideology of the Indonesian State
Penggaduhan	–	Animal husbandry tenancy system. The tenant raises cattle which he/she does not own
Usaha Bersama	–	Collective action

Thailand

Changwat	–	Province
Kwan	–	The spirit present in each and every thing
Phibob	–	Outcast, believed to be beset by evil spirits

Appendix 4: Bibliography

Anizur Rahman Kahn and Lee (eds.) (1984) – *Poverty in Rural Asia* (Bangkok: ILO/ARTEP).

Bina Desa (1985) – *Study on socio-economic grassroot organization Bina Swadaya – Usaha Bersama Case* (Jakarta: Sekretariat Bina Desa).

CENDHRRA (1982) – *The Cooperative Experience in Asian Cultures.* Workshop Report. Los Banos, The Philippines, June 1982 (Manila: Centre for the Development of Human Resources in Rural Asia).

CENDHRRA (1985) – Cendhrra Network Newsletter No. 43, 4th quarter, 1985.

COPAC – see Deane (1984).

Crombrugge, G., M. Howes and M. Nieuwkerk (1985) – *An Evaluation of CEC Small Development Projects* (Brussels: CEC, mimeo).

Deane, S. (1984) – *Cooperative Development* (Rome: COPAC).

Desroche, H. (1985) – 'La 'zone grise'. Nouvelles associations coopératives dans les pays en voie de développement'. In: *Revue des études coopératives*, no. 16, 4-ème trimestre 1985. (Paris: Fondation du Crédit Coopératif).

Van Dijk, M.P. (1986) – *Collaboration between government and non-government organisations in rural development in Sub-Sahara, Africa* (Amsterdam: Royal Tropical Institute, mimeo).

DSE (1985) – *Fighting Rural Poverty through Self-Help.* Report of an International Conference. F. van Thun and G.J. Ullrich (eds.) (Feldafing, Germany: DSE/ZEL).

El Ghonemy, R. (1985) – *The dynamics of rural poverty: An annotated outline.* FAO/DSE International Expert Consultation, Berlin, November 1985.

Emil Salim (1983) – Community Self-Help. How political is it? In: *Prisma*, no. 28, June 1983, pp. 71-73 (Jakarta: LP3ES).

ES 31 – See Osner (1986a); Osner et al. (1986b); Osner et al. (1984).

Esman, M.J. and N.T. Uphoff (1984) – *Local Organizations. Intermediaries in Rural Development.* (Ithaca, N.Y.: Cornell University Press).

FAO Consultation (1982) – Background Material of the FAO Experts' Consultation on *People's Participation in Rural Development,* held at FAO Rome, December 1982.

Galjart, B. and D. Buijs (eds.) (1982) – *Participation of the Poor in Development.* Contributions to a Seminar. Leiden Development Studies no. 2 (Leiden, the Netherlands: University of Leiden).

Guéneau, M.C. (1984) – *Analyse Economique d'un Echantillon de Petits Projets de Développement. Evaluation Ex-Post de 30 Projets situés au Sénégal et en Haute-Volta.* (Paris: Centre d'Etudes du Développement, Université de Paris).

Heijden, v.d., H. (1985) – *Development Impact and Effectiveness of Non-Governmental Organizations: The Record of Progress in Rural Development Co-operation,* OECD, Paris. Paper presented at the Symposium on 'Effectiveness of Rural Development', September 1985, Royal Tropical Institute, Amsterdam.

ILO (1984) – *Group based savings and credit for the rural poor.* Papers and proceedings of Workshop. Bogra, Bangladesh, 6-10 November, 1983 (Geneva: International Labour Office).

Ismid Hadad – Development and Community Self-Help in Indonesia. In: *Prisma,* no. 28, June 1983, pp. 3-20 (Jakarta: LP3ES).

Kilby, P. and D. D'Zmura (1985) – *Searching for Benefits.* AID Evaluation Special Study No. 28, June 1985 (Washington D.C.: U.S. Agency for International Development).

Lecompte, B. (1986) – *L'aide par projet: Limites et Alternatives* (Paris, OECD). Published in English as: *Project Aid. Limitations and alternatives.*

Lukas, H. (1983) – Bureaucracy, Participation and Distribution in Indonesian Development. In: *Prisma* no. 28, June 1983, pp. 21-32. (Jakarta: LP3ES).

Nighat Said Khan and Kamla Bhasin (1986) – Sharing on earth. Responding to the challenge of rural poverty in Asia. Role of people's organizations (Part II). In: *IFDA dossier* 54, July/August 1986, pp. 9-20 (Nyon, Switzerland).

Oakley, P. and B. Dillon (1985) – *Strengthening people's participation in rural development* (England: University of Reading).

OECD (1986) – *The Role of Non-Governmental Organizations (NGOs) in Agricultural and Rural Development in Sub-Sahara Africa.* Summary Record of the 509th meeting. 3-4 June 1986. (Paris: OECD).

Osner, K. (1986a) – Final Report of the Special Unit *'Fighting Rural Poverty through Self-Help'* (ES 31) on the second Working Phase. Part A. Report on Findings (Bonn: Federal Ministry for Economic Cooperation).

Osner, K., M. Harder, D. Rojahn, M. Schmidt-Burr, K. Schöck (1986b) – Final Report ES 31. Part B. See Osner (1986b).

Osner, K., A. Muser, K. Schöck, B. Harms, W. Schneider-Barthold (1984) – *Approaches to overcoming poverty through self-help and target-group-oriented financing instruments.* Final report of the Special Unit (S 24). (Bonn: Federal Ministry for Economic Cooperation).

Porter, D. and K. Clark (1985) – *Questioning practice: Non-government aid agencies and project evaluation.* Development Dossier no. 16 (Canberra: Australian Council for Overseas Aid).

Röling, N. and H. de Zeeuw (1983) – *Improving the Quality of Rural Poverty Alleviation.* Final Report of the Working Party on the Small Farmer and Development Cooperation (Wageningen, the Netherlands: International Agricultural Centre).

Rouille d'Orfeuil, H. (1984) – *Coopérer autrement. L'engagement des organisations non-gouvernementales aujourd'hui.* (Paris: L'Harmattan).

Schrijvers, J. (1985) – *Mothers for life. Motherhood and marginalization in the North Central Province of Sri Lanka, 1985* (Delft, the Netherlands: Eburon).

Tongsawate, M. and W.E.J. Tips (1985) – *Coordination between governmental and non-governmental organizations in Thailand's rural development.* (Bangkok: Asian Institute of Technology).

UN-ESCAP (1986) – *TCDC Workshop on Strengthening institutional credit services to low-income groups.* Summary and conclusions. Nanjing, China 26-30 May, 1986 (Bangkok: UN-ESCAP).

Verhagen, K. (1984) – *Cooperation for Survival. Analysis of an experiment in participatory research and planning with small farmers in Sri Lanka and Thailand* (Geneva: International Cooperative Alliance; Amsterdam: Royal Tropical Institute). Second print 1986.

Verhagen K. (1985) – *A comment on the S 24 study of the German Federal Ministry,* Working Document no. 1. (Oegstgeest, the Netherlands: Cebemo, mimeo).

World Bank (1980) – *The design of organizations for rural development projects.* A progress report by W.E. Smith, F.J. Lethem and B.A. Thoolen (World Bank). Draft version.

Appendix 5: Other publications produced as part of the study

Bina Swadaya (1981) – Promotion of economic activities through self-help organizations. In: *Bina Swadaya Newsletter*, no. 3 August 1986.

Bongartz H. (1986) – *The promotion of economic activities through self-help organizations. An evaluation study of self-help groups in the Special Province of Yogyakarta, Indonesia.* April 1986 (Jakarta: Bina Swadaya).

CCTD (1986) – *The promotion of economic activities in rural areas through self-help organization.* Comments on research study by Mr. Banthorn Ondam and Dr. Chattip Nortsupha during CCTD Workshop, March 1986. In: CCTD Newsletter No. 182, January-April 1986.

CEBEMO (1986a) – *Promotion of Economic Activities through self-help organizations.* Proceedings of Internal Workshop 1-6 September 1986 (restricted).

CEBEMO (1986b) – *Promotion of Economic Activities through self-help organizations.* Proceedings of Cebemo Consultation, 8, 10, 11 September 1986. (restricted).

Kaewthep, Dr. Kanjana & Dr. Kanonksak Kaewthep (1986) – *Research report on the promotion of economic activities in rural areas through self-help organizations,* April 1986 (Bangkok: CCTD).

MOC (1985) – *MOC Plan of Work 1986* (Feira de Santana: MOC, mimeo).

Oliveira F. de, J.C. de Souza Alves, J.C.B. de Santana, N. de Quintella Baptista (1986) – *Projetos Economicos Comunitarios: Estudo de uma experiença rural de Feira de Santana.* Colaboração A.M.T. de Oliveira, I.F. de Oliveira. Assessoria especial M.R. da Costa Souza, Julho – 1986 (Feira de Santana, Brazil: MOC).

Verhagen, K. (1985) – *Comment on the S 24 study: 'Approaches to overcoming poverty through self-help and target-group-oriented financial instruments'. Some reflections on the appropriateness of the financial instrument.* (Oegstgeest, the Netherlands: Cebemo, mimeo).

Appendix 6: Index of figures

Appendix 7: Index of names